1 MONTH OF
FREE
READING

at
www.ForgottenBooks.com

By purchasing this book you are eligible for one month membership to ForgottenBooks.com, giving you unlimited access to our entire collection of over 1,000,000 titles via our web site and mobile apps.

To claim your free month visit:
www.forgottenbooks.com/free920417

ISBN 978-0-265-99350-7
PIBN 10920417

Forgotten Books is a registered trademark of FB &c Ltd.
Copyright © 2018 FB &c Ltd.
FB &c Ltd, Dalton House, 60 Windsor Avenue, London, SW19 2RR.
Company number 08720141. Registered in England and Wales.

For support please visit www.forgottenbooks.com

COPYRIGHT

The copyright law of the United States - Title 17, United States Code - concerns the making of photocopies or other reproductions of copyrighted material.

Under certain conditions specified in the law, libraries and archives are authorized to furnish a photocopy or other reproduction. One of these specified conditions is that the photocopy or reproduction is not to be "used for any purpose other than private study, scholarship, or research." If a user makes a request for, or later uses, a photocopy or reproduction for purposes in excess of
"fair use," that user may be liable for copyright infringement.

This institution reserves the right to refuse to accept a copy order if, in its judgement, fulfillment of the order would involve violation of the copyright law.

FEDERAL WORKS AGENCY
WORK PROJECTS ADMINISTRATION
(Illinois)

THE CHICAGO FOREIGN LANGUAGE
PRESS SURVEY

**Translated and Compiled
by the
Chicago Public Library Omnibus Project
O.P. No. 65-1-54-273 (3)
Chicago, Illinois
1942**

INTRODUCTION

History of the Survey

In the autumn of 1936 the Chicago Foreign Language Press Survey was organized as a work project under the then Works Progress Administration of Illinois. Its purpose was to translate and classify selected news articles appearing in the foreign language press of the city during the past century. The Survey was officially sponsored by the Chicago Public Library, with the complete backing of Carl B. Roden, Librarian, and Nathan R. Levin, Assistant Librarian.

Before the project had been in existence very long, it won the support of other agencies. The Newberry Library, the Chicago Historical Society, and the John Crerar Library extended it their facilities immediately. The history departments of the University of Chicago and Northwestern University endorsed the work, and through Professors Bessie L. Pierce, Isaac J. Cox, and Tracy E. Strevey gave valuable advice and direction. The name of Professor Pierce should be singled out particularly for her splendid assistance.

The work of the Survey was also received with a lively interest by the newspapers, organizations, and leaders of the foreign language communities of the city. Not a few of them acted as co-sponsors. In fact it is no exaggeration to state that the success of the project is due in no small measure to this cooperation. Among the many newspapers and organizations that have participated, mention should be made of the following: The Abendpost, the Danish National Committee, the Danish Times, the Denni Hlasatel, the Dziennik Chicagoski, the Greek Press, the Greek Star, the Jewish Daily Courier, the Jewish Daily Forward, the Jewish People's Institute, the Národ, the Naujienos, the Polish National Alliance, the Polish Roman Catholic Union of America, the Rassviet, the Skandinaven, the Svornost, the Saloniki, and the Zgoda.

Because of a curtailment in the WPA program, the Survey was terminated in October 1941. Although it was not possible to examine all of the newspapers originally planned, the bulk of the work was completed.

The Survey was supervised at various periods by James Monaghan, Dr. Thomas R. Hall, Jane L. Cates, and George Anagnos. The gigantic task of arranging the material for microfilming was performed under the direction of George Anagnos and Oscar W. Junek.

Description of the Files

The files of the Survey consist of some 120,000 sheets (5"x8") of typewritten matter translated from newspapers of twenty-two different foreign language communities of Chicago. Represented in the Survey are the following groups:

Group	Count
Albanian	(91)
Bohemian	(15,811)
Chinese	(398)
Croatian	(1,321)
Danish	(3,847)
Dutch	(795)
Filipino	(588)
German	(18,448)
Greek	(10,706)
Hungarian	(2,688)

Italían	(2,950)
Jewish	(16,298)
Lithuanian	(5,950)
Norwegian	(7,654)
Polish	(16,368)
Russian	(5,963)
Serbian	(124)
Slovak	(509)
Slovene	(197)
Spanish	(1,909)
Swedish	(6,780)
Ukrainian	(997)

The figure appearing in parenthesis indicates the number of sheets in the files pertaining to the respective group.

For the benefit of research students, the names and dates of coverage of the principal newspapers and periodicals included in the Survey are listed below:

ALBANIAN
Albanian Journal (Monthly) 1922-23.
Albanian Messenger (Monthly) 1927-1935

BOHEMIAN
Czechoslovak Review (Monthly) 1918-24.
Denni Hlasatel (Daily) 1901-18, 1920-22.
Svornost (Daily) Apr 1878-Sep 1885, 1890-92, 1896-1900.

CHINESE
Chinese Centralist Daily News 1928.
San Min Morning Paper 1936-38.

CROATIAN
Hrvatska Zastava (Daily) 1915-17.
Hrvatski Glasnik (Weekly) 1923, 1928, 1930.
Jugoslavia (Weekly) 1921-23.
Jugoslovenska Zastava (Weekly) 1918.
Novi Svijet (Weekly) 1924-34, 1936.
Radnička Straža (Weekly) 1907-17.
Radnik (Weekly) 1923-Sep 1929.
Svjetlo (Monthly) 1911.
Znanje (Weekly) 1918-Feb 1922, 1935-36.

DANISH

Dansk Tidende (Weekly) May-Jun 1919, 1921, 1932-36.
Dansk Tidende Og Revyen (Weekly) 1922-Nov 1931.
Hejmdal (Weekly) Oct 1874-Jan 1878.
Revyen (Weekly) Apr 1895-Jun 1921.

DUTCH

Onze Toekomst (Weekly) 1906-13, 1919-27.

GERMAN

Abendpost (Daily) 1889-Sep 1911, Aug 1914-Feb 1916,
    July 1918-19, 1923-35.
Atlantis (Monthly) 1855-Apr 1858.
Chicagoer Arbeiter Zeitung (Daily) 1879-89.
Illinois Staats-Zeitung (Daily) 1861-81, 1885-1893,
    1899-1901, 1914-$_{18}$.

GREEK

American Hellenic World (Monthly) Aug 1926-Oct 1928.

GREEK (Cont'd.)
Chicago Greek Daily 1921-32, 1934-Jan 1935.
Democrat (Monthly) 1927-Apr 1931.
Greek American News (Weekly) 1936.
Greek News (Weekly) 1935.
Greek Press (Weekly) Jun 1929-Mar 1934.
Greek Star (Weekly) Jan 1908-Apr 1910.
Loxias (Weekly) Jun 1908-Nov 1918.
Proodos (Irregular) Apr 1931-Oct 1934.
Saloniki (Weekly) Aug 1913-1931.
Saloniki-Greek Press (Weekly) Mar 1934-36.
Star (Weekly) Jan 1904-Jan 1908.

HUNGARIAN
Interest (Weekly) Nov 1933, 1934-36.
Magyar Tribune (Weekly) Mar 1917-21, Jul 1924-1931,
Jan-Sep 1933.
Otthon (Weekly) 1922-36.

ITALIAN
Bollettino Della Camera Di Commercio Italiana
(Irregular) 1911-Oct 1926, Apr 1928-33, 1935-36.

ITALIAN

    Bollettino Italo-American National Union
        (Monthly) Mar 1924-36.
    Il Bollettino Sociale (Monthly) Nov 1928-Mar 1931.
    Bulletin of Illinois Grand Lodge Order of Sons of Italy in America
        (Monthly) 1927, 1930, 1932-36.
    L'Italia (Daily) Oct 1886-1920.
    Mens Italica (Monthly) 1928-29, 1936.
    La Parola del Popolo (Monthly) Sep 1921-Nov 1924.
    La Parola dei Socialisti (Weekly) 1908-May 1916.
    La Parola Prolestaria (Weekly) 1916.
    La Tribuna Italiana Transatlantica (Weekly) Jun 1904-Apr 1908.
    Vita Nuova (Monthly) 1925-31.

JEWISH

    Jewish Advance (Weekly) 1881.
    Jewish Daily Courier 1906-28.
    Jewish Daily Forward 1919-32.
    Jewish Labor World (Weekly) 1908, 1916-19.
    Jewish Standard (Weekly) Apr 1908-July 1909.

LITHUANIAN

Jaunimas (Semi-Monthly) 1926, 1930, 1936.
Katalikas (Weekly) 1899-1903.
Lietuva (Weekly) Dec 1892-1918.
Naujienos (Daily) Feb 1914-16.
Sandara (Weekly) 1930.
Vilnis (Daily) 1925-27.

NORWEGIAN

Skandia (Daily) Jun 1899-1902, 1904-08, 1910-35.
Skandinaven (Weekly) 1871-72, 1876-87, 1889-94, 1896-1921.

POLISH

Dziennik Chicagoski (Daily) 1890-97, 1903-08, 1921-22.
Dziennik Ludowy (Daily) Mar 1907-08.
Dziennik Zjednoczenia (Daily) 1921-23, 1926-30.
Dziennik Zwiazkowy Zgoda (Daily) 1908-18.
Naród Polski (Weekly) 1897-1902, 1904-21.
Polonia (Weekly) 1916-25, 1936.
Przebudzenie (Weekly) Nov 1927-31.
Zgoda (Weekly) 1887-94, 1897-1903.

RUSSIAN

Domashni Vrach (Monthly) 1916-18.
Moskva (Monthly) 1929-30.
Rassviet (Daily) May 1926-36.
Russkaya Pochta (Weekly) 1917-18.
Russkii Viestnik (Daily) Nov 1923-Apr 1926.
Russkoe Obozrenie (Monthly) 1927-30.
Svobodnaya Rossiya 1917-23.

SERBIAN

Balkan (Weekly) 1909.
Soko (Monthly) 1912-13.
Ujednijeno Srpstvo (Weekly) 1922-23, 1934, 1936.

SLOVAK

Osadné Hlasy (Weekly) Sep-Oct 1928, Mar 1929-June 1933,
    Jan 1934-Mar 1935.
Rovnost Ludu (Weekly) Oct 1906-Mar 1913.

SLOVENE

Amerikanski Slovenec (Weekly) 1925-26, 1928.
Proletarec (Weekly) 1906, 1908-13, 1915-19, 1927-1930, 1932.

SPANISH

L'Alianza (Monthly) 1936.
El Buen Samaritano (Monthly) 1924.
La Defensa (Weekly) 1935-36.
Evolución (Semi-Monthly) 1937.
El Heraldo (Weekly) 1935-1937.
Ideal (Semi-Monthly) 1929-1930.
El Ideal Católico Mexicano (Weekly) 1935-1937.
El Indicador (Weekly) 1903.
El Liberal (Bi-Monthly) 1933.
La Lucha (Semi-Monthly) 1932-1934.
El Mexicano (Weekly) 1928-1930.
Mexico (Tri-Weekly) 1928-1930.
El Nacional (Weekly) 1930-1935.
La Voz de Mexico (Monthly) 1935-1936.

SWEDISH

Svenska Amerikanaren (Weekly) 1907-1909.
Svenska Kuriren (Weekly) 1907-08, 1911-20, 1925-Sep 1929.
Svenska Nyheter (Weekly) 1903.

SWEDISH (Cont'd)
Svenska Nyheter-Humoristen (Weekly) Oct 1903-July 1906.
Svenska Tribunen (Weekly) 1878-Mar 1904, 1905-June 1906.
Svenska Tribunen-Nyheter (Weekly) July 1906-Dec 1906,
1909-1910, 1915-16, 1919-24, 1927, 1929-33.

UKRAINIAN
Nash Styah (Weekly) Dec 1933-July 1936.
Ranna Zorya (Monthly) 1919.
Sichovi Visty (Semi-Monthly) 1920-24.
Sitch (Semi-Monthly) 1924-29.
Ukraina (Weekly) May 1917-20.
Ukraina (Weekly) 1930-31.

In selecting the newspaper to be translated, availability was the chief determining factor. Since the publication dates of no one newspaper coincided with the life of a particular foreign language community, it was necessary to use several papers to obtain complete coverage. In several instances, however, two papers with widely divergent views covering the same period were examined.

The material for each foreign language group is arranged separately. Within each group the sheets are filed in reverse chronology with the most recent date first, and under the following code outline:

I. ATTITUDES
    A. Education
        1. Secular
            a. Elementary, Higher (High School and College)
            b. Foreign Languages
            c. Taxation for Public Schools
            d. Special Endowments
        2. Parochial
            a. Elementary, Higher (High School and College)
            b. Foreign Languages
            c. Contributions
            d. Special Endowments
        3. Adult Education

E. Social Organization
F. Politics
    1. Voting as Blocs
    2. Part Played by Social and Political Societies
    3. Programs and Purposes
    4. Extent of Influence
    5. Political Leadership
    6. Graft and Corruption
G. War
H. Social Problems and Social Legislation
 J. Interpretation of American History
K. Position of Women and Feminism
L. Agriculture in the United States
M. Health and Sanitation
II. CONTRIBUTIONS AND ACTIVITIES
A. Vocational
    1. Professional
    2. Industrial and Commercial
    3. Aesthetic
       a. Arts and Handicrafts

        b. Music
        c. Painting and Sculpture
        d. Theatrical
            (1) Drama
            (2) Dancing
    B. Avocational and Intellectual
        1. Aesthetic
            a. Music
            b. Painting and Sculpture
            c. Theatrical
                (1) Drama
                (2) Dancing
                (3) Festivals, Pageants, Fairs and Expositions
            d. Literary Societies
            e. Literature
        2. Intellectual
            a. Libraries
            b. Museums
            c. Scientific and Historical Societies

It was not intended that this outline be a rigid classification scheme. The headings were made sufficiently general so that large varieties of material could be easily grouped together. At the same time the outline follows what is considered a logical development from the point of view of subject content. It is hoped that this arrangement will facilitate the use of the files.

Alex Ladenson
Project Supervisor

The Chicago Public Library Omnibus Project
Work Projects Administration
1400 W Washington Blvd.
Chicago, Ill.

CGP 2004.001.15: Danish, II D10 (February 24, 1912) – V B

CGP 2004.001.16: Dutch, I A1a – II D5

CGP 2004.001.17: Dutch, II D8 – V A1

CGP 2004.001.18: Filipino, I A1a – V B

CGP 2004.001.19: German, I A1a – I B1 (April 16, 1881)

CGP 2004.001.20: German, I B1 (April 2, 1881) –
I D2a (2) (December 14, 1891)

CGP 2004.001.21: German, I D2a (2) (December 14, 1891) –
I F1 (October 4, 1872)

CGP 2004.001.22: German, I F1 (August 7, 1872) – I F6

CGP 2004.001.23: German, I G – I H (February 17, 1919)

CGP 2004.001.24: German, I H (February 13, 1919) – II A3c

CGP 2004.001.25: German, II A3d (1) –
II B1c (3) (September 13, 1880)

CGP 2004.001.26: German, II B1c (3) (September 5, 1880) –
II D1 (January 9, 1901)

CGP 2004.001.27: German, II D1 (December 17, 1897) –
III A (October 22, 1915)

CGP 2004.001.28: German, III A (September 6, 1915) –
III C (September 26, 1879)

CGP 2004.001.29: German III C June 11 1879 –

III C (November 16, 1933)

THIS REEL CONTAINS:

CGP 2004-001.79

Slovene

I A2a - IV

<u>List of Irregularities:</u>

-Image quality in original uneven throughout

-Index of topics are found in the upper left corner of frame

-Some titles appear in microfilm but were not included in INDEX of titles

Revision Statement

The original film was made from the holdings of the Chicago Public Library by the University of Chicago Libraries, Department of Photographic Reproductions. In 2004 it was reorganized and direct duplicated by OCLC Preservation Service Center to better meet current preservation standards and to better assist patrons in their research.

2. Parochial
   a. Elementary, Higher (High
      School and College)

I A 2 a   SLOVENE
I C
          Amerikanski Slovenec, Vol. XXXVII, No. 171, Sept. 6, 1928.

                        SCHOOL IN SOUTH CHICAGO

It came as a big surprise to people who know how hard it is to unite us
Slavs, but it is the truth that in South Chicago we Slovenes and Croats
work shoulder to shoulder.

As a result of such harmony, just a few weeks ago in South Chicago we
opened a new school, which has already about 250 children enrolled. If
only our people come to their senses and forget their political, religious
and national differences, this cooperation can be found in other ways, as
economics and education.

This example can be followed by other colonies, for the benefit of their
members. Why our children must travel so far to their schools, as has been
the case with children in South Chicago, who made daily trips to Calumet
City, or must enroll in a Catholic school, where religion is the major
subject.

I A 2 a
II B 1 c (3)

Amerikanski Slovenec, Vol. XXXV, No. 191, October 2, 1926.

CARNIVAL OF ST. STEPHAN

We all know well that without our support the Slovene Catholic schools cannot exist. We do not need to tell you, people, here that our schools in Chicago badly need our support, and that it is our duty to extend a helping hand.

Therefore we invite you all to come next Saturday to a Catholic carnival, where we will double our joy by entertainment and by enlisting in the lives of benefactors of our schools.

I A 2 a   SLOVENE
I A 1 a

Amerikanski Slovenec, Vol. XXXIV, No. 134, Aug. 26, 1925.

SEND YOUR CHILDREN TO A CATHOLIC SCHOOL

Our church holds itself responsible for the spiritual welfare of its
members and insists that the same responsibility should be applied in
the religious relationship between Catholic parents and their children.
People are the children of the Catholic Church, and why should not the
church responsibility be followed in the case of parents and their offspring? We believe that everybody understands the value of religious
education for our children.

If it is true that only parents brought up in the spirit of the Catholic
religion can educate their children rightly, it is also true that only
Catholic schools can give the children the right kind of education.

The only objection against sending children to Catholic schools, as we
know, is the small fee of 50 cents a month which these schools charge.
This is the reason why Catholic parents send their children to public
schools instead of Catholic schools. Public schools are good in every

Amerikanski Slovenec, Vol. XXXIV, No. 134, Aug. 26, 1925.

respect, but they do not offer the Catholic discipline which is of so
great importance in building the child's character.

There is no better place in the world to get religious education than
the Catholic schools.

Parents, we warn you of your responsibilities as members of the Catholic
Church, and hope that our voice will be heard and the church rules obeyed.

Amerikanski Slovenec, Vol. XXXIV, No. 92, June 12, 1925.

NEW CATHOLIC COLLEGE IN LEMONT, ILLINOIS

We, Slovenes in America, do not have so many cultural institutions. Next Sunday, June 14, we can consider as a day of great importance for all Slovenes in America, and especially for our people living in the small town of Lemont, Illinois.

On this memorable day our people in this town will have a happy occasion to witness the brilliant celebration of the opening of the institution, the only one of its kind in America, the new Catholic College of St. Francis. We have not enough words to describe fully the great importance of this cultural institution, its role to be played in cultural life of our people, not only in Lemont, but in all places of this country where our people exist. We believe that the opening of this institution will start a new era in our life.

The main purpose of this college is to give our people highly educated spiritual leaders and priests. Also to build a center from where culture

I A 2 a   · 2 ·   <u>SLOVENE</u>

Amerikanski Slovenec, Vol. XXXIV, No. 92, June 12, 1925.   WPA (ILL) PROJ 30275

will be radiating among our people. This institution has also other
noble ideals, as to guard our religious standard from our enemy, who
is doing its destructive work from its nest in Lawndale Street, Chicago.
Religion is a great power and necessity in our life, and everybody who
works against such power is really offering very bad service to our people.

A. Education
   3. Adult Education

I A 3
II B 2 f
II B 2 g

SLOVENIAN

Proletarec, Vol. 13, No. 1076, April 26, 1928.

EDUCATIONAL DEPARTMENT OF JUGOSLAV SOCIALIST FEDERATION

The purpose and activities of the Educational Division of the Jugoslav Socialist
Federation have been outlined a number of times before. Still there is that
clamoring for more information from many of our friends. We have decided,
therefore, to give a brief and accurate account below, paying particular attention to the necessity of education to all the workers, and especially to the
Jugoslavs.

Education is the prime factor of all progress. If you go back into the dark
ages, you will find that those races that adopted newer, more practical methods
as a result of many experiments, held the controling power of the earth. The
early centuries produced the forward looking elements of Greek and Roman philo-
sophers who lifted their races above those of the barbarians. But leave what
is gone, behind. Education today is a necessity. It is necessary that you
study and learn daily because you may have work today, but tomorrow you might
be obliged to look for it elsewhere. You must know what you are doing because,
after all, you are selling for a small salary your ability, which in turn de-
pends upon your knowledge - that is your answer. Education is your means of

Proletarec, Vol. 13, No. 1076, April 26, 1928.

securing food and shelter so that your body may live. It is just as essential
as food and clothing.

Not only should you know and learn more about your daily earning power; you must
also know and learn about the wonderful human mechanism, your system. What to
do and what not to do when sickness overtakes you; what is good and what is bad
for it.

To keep in constant touch with the world, you must read and study periodicals,
books, etc., just as most of you must follow the procedures of your fraternal
societies to know what it is doing or what it contemplates to do.

There are countless numbers of features about which we know very little. You
must know art to love it - song to admire it; but more attention to it together
with your incessant desire to know, to learn, will bring art closer to your eyes
and song closer to your ears.

It has been conceded so often that centralization of all groups and organization
enables and permits them to function better, and that all such centralized work
is less expensive. One group can do little, but one hundred groups united can

Proletareo, Vol. 13, No. 1076, April 26, 1928.

do muoh; because separate groups operating alone would gain less exerting the same amount of energy than a centralized union of many such groups.

The Jugoslav Socialist Federation under date of November of 1921, organized this Central Educational Division for the purpose of:

First: (a) Supply such literature which would eventually persuade its readers to look toward the future, even though we perish without securing that for which we crave.

(b) Literature which will describe the vast natural resources and the powers that now exploit it, with the tendency and argument that this world with all its beauty, power, and raw material, rightfully belongs to you, who work from day to day to make it bigger and better, as much as it does to those who have done nothing, but still claim it.

Second: (a) By elevating our social lives to greater heights; teaching and encouraging plays of meaning and benefit, as well as plays of amusement. For, after all, a worker needs to laugh to keep fit, much more than a non-producer.

(b) Supporting those musically inclined to satisfy their hearts' great-

Proletarec, Vol. 13, No. 1076, April 26, 1928.

est desire to keep on singing merrily in spite of our many hardships. Life without musio - would there be any?

Third: (a) To arrange and prepare lectures.
       (b) Disoussions.
       (c) Debates.

People of our race will much more readily comprehend our views when a fluent speaker addresses them with knowledge and gesture - one who has a sincere desire to help people understand, giving everyone an equal opportunity to express his viewpoints on questions of vital importance.

Fourth: To inspire, teach, and uphold the truth above everything else in spite of all our handicaps.

The Educational Division of the Jugoslav Socialist Federation has supplied literature which is fit to read and has helped in the uplift of our social, dramatic, and musical lives. It has prepared lectures, discussions, and debates for the past seven years, and its membership grows each year; for as the work expands, it speaks for itself. It is self-evident that from the growth of about forty

Proletareo, Vol. 13, No. 1076, April 26, 1928.

organizations, contributing the first year to one hundred and six organizations for 1927, ours is a worthy cause deserving all the support you and your branch can give it.

While it is true that much of this material may be obtained at school, it is also true that our Jugoslav race has had but an inkling of it. You are one of us; it is your duty to yourself and to your friends to work in behalf of this educational division. It is not too late to enroll for 1928. Address all correspondence to Mr. Charles Pogareleo, 3639 W. 26th St., Chicago, Ill.

I. ATTITUDES
    B. Mores
        2. Blue Laws

Amerikanski Slovenec, Vol. XXXV, No. 39, Feb. 17, 1926.

PEOPLE'S SENTIMENT AGAINST PROHIBITION

For the past seven years the American people have been feeling the taste of prohibition. This law was enacted during the war and its enforcement is getting tougher. Prohibition is commonly known as the Volsted Act; it acquired this name from Senator Volsted, who was the father of the Act.

It is a known fact that this Act was not accepted so cheerfully by the drinking public, and Volsted has been cursed by this class of people, but still Volsted eagerly defended his Act. He sincerely believed that by enforcement of this Act, the country would greatly benefit by eliminating lots of evils. He also believed that his Act would cut down heavy drinking, but he overlooked the fact that prohibition developed such enormous corruptions that government and people really got to thinking which was better: corruption of free drinking.

Seven years of prohibition experience shows us that despite strong

Amerikanski Slovenec, Vol. XXXV, No. 32, Feb. 17, 1926.

enforcement of the Volsted Act, we in America have as many drunkards
as it was registered before prohibition era. On another side it is
already a proven fact that thousands of innocent people paid with
their lives enjoying bootleg liquors of various kinds.

During the prohibition era a great many enormous and small fortunes
are made. "Beer flats" and "big shots" of lawbreaking organizations
developed the system of bribing police, and without any interference
were selling openly "poison drinks" for the prices from 25 to 75 cents.

No wonder that a great many millionaires with an army of hoodlums were
reaping profits.

The Catholic Church teaches people to be humble. It preaches to its
followers that being humble is the greatest asset in character. Over-

<u>SLOVENIAN</u>

<u>Amerikanski Slovenec</u>, Vol. XXXV, No. 32, Feb. 17, 1926.

drinking can be considered as a debit in good character; it is a sin against religion.

Our church leaders openly opposed prohibition, which become cow for numberless politicians, officials and bootleggers. Prohibition in a form as it exists nowadays, is nothing more than a sort of fanaticism and as such will not bear wholesome fruits. The people in their majority, especially people of Slav extraction, are against prohibition.

I. ATTITUDES
    C. Own and
        Other National
        Or Language Groups

I C   SLOVENIAN
III C
I A 2 a
        Amerikanski Slovenec, Vol. XXXVII, No. 171, Sept. 6, 1928.

/CROATIAN AND SLOVENIAN SCHOOLS/

It is pleasant to know that Croats and Slovenes united together in religious and social work in South Chicago. As a result of this cooperation
we have a new church building with a school, which has over 250 children
already. Just a few blocks away we have another school of St. Patrick's
Church. This school has 320 children. There is also St. Jury's School, with
a large number of children enrolled. Our schools have, beside Slovenian
and Croatian children, also Polish, Slovak and Italian. All these nationalities heartily support our church and school. This just shows that great
work can be done if all our people get together and forget their mis-
understandings. At least our school problem is solved to a certain extent,
so far as South Chicago is concerned.

It was really hard for our children to walk or ride every day to the
Calumet Public School, and now when we have three schools of our own,
children will enjoy school work and save their energy.

I. ATTITUDES
   D. Economic
      Organization
      2. Labor Organization & Activities
         a. Unions
            (4) Strikes

Proletarec, Vol. 5, No. 170, December, 13, 1910.

HELP THE STRIKE!

<u>The Daily Socialist</u> issued an extra number for the benefit of tailors on strike in Chicago. The net profit from the sale of this extra issue, as well as moral support, will be offered to the strikers.

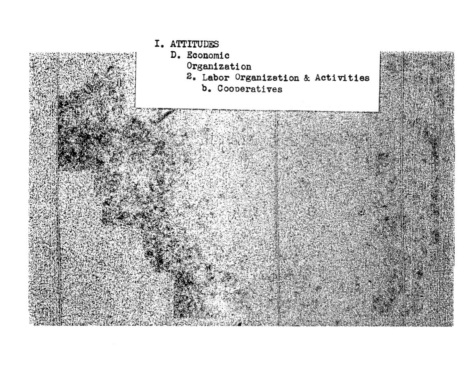

I. ATTITUDES
   D. Economic
      Organization
      2. Labor Organization & Activities
         b. Cooperatives

Proletarec, Vol. 6, No. 212, Oct. 3, 1911.

SOUTH SLAVIC COOPERATIVE PRINTING ESTABLISHMENT.

A charter for a South Slavic Cooperative Printing Establishment has been issued and registered in Cook County on the seventh day of September under No. L824970.

This charter shows that the aforenamed establishment will issue stock of one thousand dollars per share with a maximum capitalization of ten thousand dollars.

I. ATTITUDES
    D. Economic
       Organization
       2. Labor Organization &
          Activities
          c. Unemployment

Amerikanski Slovenec, Vol. XXXVII, No. 17,   Jan. 26, 1928.

SLOVENIAN RELIEF ORGANIZATION

Collections for the unemployed have been received in the church of St.
Stjefen, and brought a sum of $240. Gifts are received daily. Our relief
organization is working hard in order to meet the great need. This organization is planning to open branches.

Headquarters for this relief organization have been established at 1852
W. 22nd Place, Chicago.

Chicago and vicinity are showing deep interest in this noble action.

Branch managers are asked to send their reports daily in order to coordinate
the fast growing and complicated work.

Amerikanski Slovenec, Vol. XLVII, No. 8, Jan. 11, 1922. WPA (ILL) PROJ 30275

CARE DUE TO THE UNEMPLOYED

Unemployment nowadays is as bad with Slovenes as with a great many people in America. We Slovenes, it seems, have been hit harder than people of any other nationality for the simple reason that the majority of our people are employed in two major industries: steel and coal mines. Both above named industries are suffering hard from lack of production, so workers get laid off daily and (are) thrown on the streets.

The coming winter surely will bring a lot of sorrow, and even tragedy, to our people. Those who have been hit by the depression or suffer from lack of employment must be helped, and that help must come first from us. Last Saturday St. Stjefan Society invited all Slovenes in Chicago to be present on a special meeting, where plans for relief to the unemployed will be discussed.

We Slovenes always have been known as a people with kind hearts, and we sincerely believe that on this occasion our help will come quickly and sufficiently.

SLOVENIAN

Majskiglas, (The May Herald), May 1937.　　WPA (ILL) : : : : 30271

OUR PAST AND FUTURE

Although it is impossible to forget, we can and should disregard our
diversified folly during the entire lifetime of the modern Socialist
movement throughout the world. By "disregard" I mean that we should
let bygones be bygones except for what we can learn from them, and
throw overboard all grudges we have accumulated against each other
during all these years in factional battles under different realms,
while believing fundamentally, practically in the same principles as
to what must be our future social order, to render equality, justice
and international tranquillity to all mankind.

The main economic question is to change from private ownership of
natural and produced wealth to Socialism, under such regulations
that everyone from twenty to sixty years of age who is able-bodied
and willing to work will have a position with enough earnings to
be able to acquire all the necessities of life, and the government
will take care of the disabled, sick, minors and the old and provide

Majskiglas, May 1937.

them with sufficient income to be able to enjoy life.

The machinery of production and transportation is at present so highly developed that if properly applied to relieve the physical work of man, a workday to produce the necessities of life would be only three or four hours long.

Since nothing is impossible, this will come in due time. But what will the world do with it if it retains the present social order? Unemployment, comparing our present state of things to the future highly developed mechanism when man's physical endeavor will be spared, even button pressing will be replaced by telepathy, would increase to at least ninety per cent of the entire population of the globe. That would create unbespeakable starvation on one side, and a wild search for markets by private capitalists on the other.

Consequently, all capitalistic countries would be constantly engaged

in hostile international strife; war after war would be declared by
masters to conquer new world markets, and all the fighting would be
done by the economically enslaved people that have nothing to fight
for. To escape such tragedy we must take in due time proper steps
to eliminate all causes for international hate by expropriation of
political power and economic wealth, and then establish the new social
order of justice, peace and universal tranquillity. Thinking about
this I distinctly remember what our late comrade, E. V. Debs, in
a fiery speech in Chicago after his release from a federal prison
bluntly and defiantly declared: "I wouldn't go to a capitalistic
war at the point of a bayonet!"

Let that be well remembered by our younger generation. Fratricide
in our schismatic political struggles is the worst curse we can
indulge in in our organizational endeavor to unify mental and physical workers of the world.

Let us discard this in favor of a new and more plausible motto: "With

Majskiglas, May 1937.   wr... ... ...

malice toward none who believe in our fundamental principles of social-
ization and equal distribution of national income." In unifying the
working class we will be inconceivably more successful through fraternal
tolerance than we have been heretofore by our condemnable schismatic
quarreling in factional divisions, trying to impose on each other our
different petty opinions that should not, and in fact do not, change
the basic idea of the whole economic scheme on which the entire new
social order will be built.

Spread this doctrine by press and spoken word throughout the land,
build up our newspapers and local organizations, and we will have
a unified international, fighting, political organization.

Let us dedicate ourselves wholeheartedly to support the Socialist
ideals till our battle is won for all humanity. Let us shorten the
distance between now and the dawn of our emancipation by united action.

Majskiglas, May 1937.

Crush private capitalism and establish a new social order; this is
our most pertinent task to accomplish during our lives.

Frank S. Pauchar.

I F
IN... S d (1)

Lojski Glass (The Herald), Vol. XI, p. 10, May 1935.

THE SOUL AND LIBERTY

This year's issue of the Lay Herald is a jubilee number, dedicated to the 30th anniversary of our weekly, Proletarec.

This occasion is rare, because very few Socialist paper were able to struggle along for such a length of time. Our paper succeeded. Now it goes into its fourth decade, young in its inspiration, full of pep and with determination to continue its battle for the interest of the workers.

Proletarec has witnessed a great number of publications succumb. Foreign language groups of the Socialist movement, with few exceptions, lost ground and some disappeared.

The Slovenes, who are one of the smallest nationalities in this country and who in the period after the war constituted 90% of the leadership

- 2 -

Majski Glass (May Herald), Vol. XV, p. 50, May 1935.

in the Jugoslav Socialist Federation, are relatively the strongest
foreign language section in the American Socialist movement. Only the
Finnish Federation could show a better picture than ours. After the
World War the American Socialist Party was completely destroyed in
many localities. Our branches then replaced the Socialist Party for
a few years in quite a few places, especially in Western Pennsylvania,
Michigan, Northern Minnesota, Eastern Ohio, and even in Cleveland and
Detroit, until the general movement was revived.

It was not our ambition to play this leading part. This situation
affected our movement rather in a very harmful way, because the bulk
of the membership was discouraged. If Americans don't care, why should
"we spent our money and time?" inquired many of our comrades.

Here and there an American branch was established. Our comrades thought
that they would be an encouragement to them, but instead they asked for
support, mostly financial support.

I R   · C   SLOVENIAN

II E S d (1)   WPA (ILL.) PROJ 30275

Majski Glas (May Herald), Vol. IV, p. 30, May 1944.

This situation gradually discouraged a great number of our members, who then became passive or even withdrew from the movement. Others continued with their work, believing in the historical mission of the Socialist movement so much that they could not resign from the task under any circumstances.

Beside the Finns there is no other nationality in America in which the Socialist movement, proportionately, is as firmly established as in ours. That is the result of the 30-year work of our branches and their paper, Proletarec. In conclusion, let it be stated that we always worked for the unity of the labor movement. Our task is to help build a Socialist movement, not quarreling factions. This is the purpose Proletarec and our federation are serving. We are in battle for a bigger and better Socialist party, for building the Socialist press. This was the aim of Proletarec 30 years ago. It still is and it will be until our final victory.

                                   Frank Leitz.

I E
II D 2 d (1)

Nyshi Glas (New Herald), Vol. XI, p. 1, May 1955.

THROUGH THE PEOPLE'S FRATERNAL REGARD

The American Socialist movement has great cause and its heartiest fraternal greetings to Proletarec in its 30th year of publication.

Through Proletarec the Socialist Party of the United States of America greets the Jugoslav comrades who have shown such a great spirit of self-sacrifice, enthusiasm, devotion and loyalty to the Socialist cause. In a movement where sacrifices on the part of workers are everywhere prevalent, it is still necessary to point out the special sacrifices made by the pioneers who founded Proletarec and kept it alive until it could stand on its own feet.

The struggles of Proletarec reflected the struggles of the American-born Socialists to keep their organization alive in spite of war, post-war prosecutions, the insanity of Communist splits, and then the complacency of prosperity.

III C 3 (1)
    Majakfiles (Daily Herald), Vol. XI, p. 21, May 1935.

Fortunately, the American movement is now coming of age and is throwing off the leading strings which the years of exile had brought.

During 1934 there was more literary Socialist works than any other year since 1920, with the exception of a national campaign year of 1932.

More pamphlets and leaflets were distributed, more radio speeches were given, more outstanding speakers ranted, and more organizers toured than in any other comparable period since the war.

The American movement, which for a long while had to lean heavily upon the arms of the foreign comrades, now is able to strike out ahead on its own strength and responsibility. Only five or six years ago the foreign language federations of the party included fifty-five percent of its membership. Today the foreign language federations have increased

Majski Glas (May Herald), Vol. XV, p. 51, May 1935.

their workers, but because of a much greater increase in the English-speaking ranks the foreign language federations represent only 10% of the Socialist Party's total membership.

The party has three times as large a proportion of industrial workers in its ranks as the country as a whole. Increasingly, the farmers of America are becoming interested in Socialism and enrolling under the Socialist banner. The outstanding work done by the party in the defense of the union officials of this and in the organization and defense of the newly-organized Southern Tenant Farmers' Union have been outstanding instances of the party's fine work.

The party is on the road to success. With the splendid cooperation that the Jugoslav comrades have shown, with the heroic team work on the part of the thousands of new recruits that have come into the movement in the past few years, we will have in America Socialism in our time.

Florence Senior.

American Slovenec, Vol. XXXIV, No. 10, Jan. 20, 1935.   WPA (ILL. PROJ. 30275

AMERICAN SLOVENEC AGAINST SOCIALISM

It is a well known fact that our Slavic people is the hardest to agree
with other people's opinion, no matter what question is put up. We will
stubbornly stick to our opinion, even if we perfectly understand that
such opinion is wrong.

The study of our people here, in America, convinces us that a great many
changes have been made under the moon, but our character and our nature
of being stubborn remained unchanged, despite new customs, circumstances,
etc.

Here is a plain illustration: Right here, in America, we have over
200,000 people of our race, but believe it or not, a group of 700 Socialists want to rule our entire population. Of course, we will resist and
we will win our political freedom, but at the same time we are not sur-
prised at all at the courage of the socialists when we see so much disagreement and deep misunderstanding existing among our leaders. This

American Slovenec, Vol. XXXIV, No. 10, Jan. 20, 1935.

disagreement has no base, and is nothing more than a result of a play of
"who will outsmart who?" But the masses must, as usual, pay for this.

We are sincerely warning our leaders that it will be in their interest
as well, as it will bring lots of good to our community if they stop
harmful egoistic propaganda; otherwise the undesirable Socialists will
really gain influence among our people.

I E
I F 6
I D 2 c

SLOVENIAN

WPA (ILL.) PROJ. 30275

Proletarec, Vol. 27, No. 1285, May-Day Issue, 1932.

OUR JOB FOR SOCIALISM

All over the world, except Russia, exists the most bitter economic and industrial depression in the history of mankind. Millions of workers have become
victims of want in lands of abundant foodstuffs and all other needs.

In the United States alone, approximately 10,000,000 workers have no employment.
Our governing powers make as adequate measures for relief as the situation
grows worse. Primary elections of the Republican and Democratic parties again
confirm the belief that politicians were not concerned about the vital issue
of unemployment that is driving the people to desperation and starvation. Their
object was to get elected by exposing their opponents to graft, corruption, and
showing what bitter enemies they were to the working class.

It is the old traditional game of mud-slinging; but when a third party arises,
both Republican and Democratic parties unite under a camouflage of non-partisan-
ship and fight desperately against any movement of the working class.

Within the next few weeks presidential candidates for the Fall election will be
nominated. Every effort will be made to get the support of the people for the
crooked politicians. Huge sums of money will be squandered for campaign purposes.

Proletarec, Vol. 27, No. 1285, May-Day Issue, 1932.

Some candidates spend ten times more money to get elected than the salary brings.
What is the purpose of this mad scramble for office?

Surely these would-be friends of labor are not going to serve the interests of the
people who contribute for the people who contribute nothing to their campaign
chests, but instead will support their financial backers for the large donations
and personal interests. This has proved to be a fact time and again; and when
the great mass of workers lose patience with one administration, they flock to
support the other. Due to their inability to see, they do not realize that both of
the old parties are owned and controled by the capitalist class.

It is futile to hope for anything better while they are at the helm.

"Of all times, this is one time when every American Socialist should be on the
job, building socialist circulation, socialist organization", said a columnist
in the American Guardian not long ago.

We can not stress too highly this important work for our movement. In the midst
of all misery and hardship that people must suffer under capitalism, they are
today more willing to listen to our message; and the need is greater than ever

WPA (ILL) PROJ 3027F

Proletarec, Vol. 27, No. 1285, May-Day Issue, 1932.

for such work in the coming elections.

In some states the Socialist party is not a legal party, because laws have been enacted which demand an outrageous percentage of votes to get on the ballot. This is another burden we must overcome. Petitions signed by citizens who did not vote at primary elections are the only road open for us. Each and every comrade will be called upon by the party to join this army of solicitors.

With the cooperation of all, we look forward to a new society to replace the present broken down regime, which benefits the few while millions of workers are left to look out for themselves. We will not only accomplish our goal, but demonstrate an impressive demand upon the money lords that the people are well aware of who are responsible for the existing conditions.

Branches of J.S.F. will also find plenty to do in the next few months. Several of our comrades in different states have been nominated on the Socialist ticket. Plans will have to be arranged for public meetings and speakers.

Circulrs and leaflets will have to be distributed to call the attention of work- ers to our cause. Every comrade - yes, the young folks too, must volunteer for

Proletarec, Vol. 27, No. 1285, May-Day Issue, 1932 WPA (ILL. ... 3027

this duty and help carry on the work. Victory for our cause will not be hand-
ed to us. We must organize, plan our campaign, and bring the issues to the
public.

Socialist victories in Milwaukee, West Allis, Racine and other cities in Wisconsin were by no means easy to attain. Opponents, financed by business enter-
prises, the powerful press, representing the interests of capitalists, the radio,
and all other agencies, used by politicians to uphold the system to benefit
their masters, waged a bitter battle against the common people.

This is a fine example of what can be done and must be done to bring about a
change in the society that will be of, for and by the working class.

The present system of capitalism will destroy itself just as feudalism and chat-
tel slavery passed out of existence, and a higher social order will take its
place. Only through effective political and industrial organization of all
people can we hasten its extinction. Comrades, let's face this task squarely,
do our duty so that we may have and enjoy Socialism in our time.

Let's rally under its banners and join hands with the workers in the great cause

Proletarec, Vol. 27, No. 1285, May-Day Issue, 1932.

for the cooperative commonwealth. On this May-Day let us rejoice over what
has already been accomplished, and renew our enthusiasm for our work until the
goal is reached.

John Rak.

SLOVENIAN

Proletarec, Vol. 25, No. 1191, May 1, 1930.   WPA (ILL.) PROJ. 30275

JUGOSLAV POLITICAL.

The Jugoslav Socialist Federation had its beginning in 1900, when the first Socialist branch of Slovene workers was organized in Chicago. Its members took the
leading part in establishing a corporation, starting with a paper, which was
friendly to the Socialist movement and mainly educational in purpose.

The task for them at the time was too heavy and the result therefore a failure.
The branch was dissolved for two years. However, in 1903 the branch was restored
and has been active ever since. With the appearance of Proletarec in 1906 and
even before, because of the help of the weekly, Glas Svobode, other branches
sprung up in various Slovene settlements.

In 1906 and 1907 advanced workers of the Croat and Serb nationalities organized
themselves in the Socialist branches. In December 1909 a preparatory conference
was held in Chicago for the purpose of establishing a Jugoslav Socialist Federation.
All Jugoslav nationalities were represented (Slovene, Croat, Serb, and Bulgarian).

Proletarec, Vol. 25, No. 1181, May 1, 1930.

The first convention was held July 4 and 5, 1910 in Chicago, at which time the Federation was born.

Mahlone Barnes represented the Socialist Party at this conference.

The growth of the Federation after its inception was very fast. During and after the war, however, many critical situations occurred. Our membership dwindled, branches disappeared, and two publications were lost. One, because it changed to a communistic paper, and the other was discontinued. Proletarec remained; advancing the cause, represented by the Federation.

It survived those stormy days and continued its struggle in the interest of the workers. Its eighth regular convention will be held in Detroit, Michigan, May 30 being the opening date. It will be in session three days.

The future looks bright, because it belongs to the Socialist movement and Socialism.

SLOVENIAN

Amerikanski Slovenec, Vol. XXXV, No. 69, April 9, 1926.

COMMUNISTS ARE BRIBING WORKERS' PRESS

The Communists are trying hard to bring themselves close to the working class and we must give them credit for being very unscrupulous every time they want to pull a lie. We heard the confidential news that Communists organized a new press bureau, whose aim is to propagate, print, and distribute articles, with the keynote as to how the working class in Russia enjoys heavenly privileges. In fact we and the majority of the world know that these stories and propaganda are ridiculous, full of lies, but still Communists are steadily pounding the same motive.

As an example of this ridiculous propaganda we will ask the readers' attention to a recently published article which was trying to employ statistics as a convincing fact of the workers' heavenly life in Russia.

Among other things painting workers' life we found that Communists proudly state that in Russia there are over 7,000,000 registered Communists. We must admit our skepticism concerning Communists' rights

SLOVENIAN

Amerikanski Slovenec, Vol. XXXV, No. 69, April 9, 1926.

to rule and regulate the life of 165,000,000 Russians. We believe that
this country, with 120,000,000 population, will be a bit worried of
having communistic rule or even influence, if we have 7,000,000 Communists here.

Now comes the employment situation. This situation, no matter how much
colorful paint be spent by the government-guided press, doesn't look
so brilliant. Of course, very obliging Communist writers did not over-
look the question of workers wages, which looks so big on paper but
do not mean very much in everyday life, if we just compare existing
prices. With all will to believe that communistic workers' heaven
really exists, we hardly find trace of it, despite such bribes as
the Communist Press Bureau.

Amerikanski Slovenec, Vol. XXXIV, No. 26, Feb. 18, 1925.

CAPITALISTS AGAIN DECLARE WAR AGAINST WORKERS

The armistice between capitalists and workers did not last very long. The
short-lived peace came to an end. Strongly organized capitalism declared
war on the hard working class, which is trying to make an honest living.
This time capitalists found it necessary to put high pressure on the
miners' union, and in all probability the capitalists will win again.
The disorganized working class will hardly resist the underground diplo-
matic work of capitalists who do the best to employ the brightest brains
in order to smash the workers' fully justified resistance and their fight
for honest existence.

In this war a capitalist never overlooks even the dirtiest means to conquer the working class. The capitalist feel perfectly happy when they keep
miners underground, where day is turned into night.

It is time for the workers to realize the priceless value of workers' unity
and solid organization, if they want to become winners instead of being

Amerikanski Slovenec, Vol. XXXIV, No. 26, Feb. 18, 1925.

always the losers.

Working conditions in all branches of industrial life, especially in the
mining industry, is gettting worse, and almost unbearable. Something has
to be done, and this something, in our honest opinion, is the campaign
for unionization with strong support from the workers. Workers also must
appeal to the government to stop giving support to capitalists.

I E
I A 1 a
III C

SLOVENIAN

Proletarec, Mar. 27, 1919.

SOCIALISM AND SCHOOLS

Socialism is the main ideal which is to break down the great difference
existing between the capitalists and the working class. It must fight
for the equal education of the workers' children also.

Capitalists are doing their best to provide the best education for their
children, but the workers' children are obtaining education mostly from
public schools.

Capitalistic schools are teaching their pupils Science and distributing
practical knowledge, but the workers' children are "fed" with fairy stories
from the Old Testament.

A long time ago, People's schools became ineffective so far as their program

Proletarec, Mar. 27, 1919.

was concerned, and more and more adapted their program to serve the purpose of the capitalists', because, as the old proverb says: "It is easier
to rule the masses when they are ignorant."

Socialism did **not** see children as future slaves of the capitalist regime,
but as full-**fledged** and equal members of society. Socialism is against
capitalistic culture, which is depriving the workers' class of its rights to
live intelligently and comfortably.

Schools in capitalistic countries are grooming reaction and **military** culture.

Socialism, on the contrary, is striving to put the schools in the service of liberty
democracy, **and** strives to make them free in all grades from grammar school
to college.

Socialism strives to make the present day schools Socialistic.

SLOVENIAN

Proletarec, Mar. 27, 1919.

Feudal masters in the Middle Ages kept the schools with the main idea of developing good citizens of the feudal regime. Capitalistic governments of today have united their efforts with the church influence, and are doing everything possible to educate the masses to be obedient church followers, tireless workers, and soft material for exploitation. For this last reason, capitalistic schools are in open war with the working class.

The pious element should be entirely removed from the school program, because the general purpose of the school is to teach Science, which will help us to improve our lives right here in this world, but not to prepare us for an imaginary life in the sky.

The purpose of the school is to give the people practical knowledge, but the schools of today are dominated with the idea of distributing theoretical and practically worthless information.

SLOVENIAN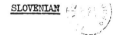

Proletarec, Mar. 27, 1919.

Professional education is what the workers need badly. This type of
education will give us an opportunity to develop skill and gain knowledge
in several lines, and make it easier for us to find jobs. In the situation
as it exists now-a-days, a minority of skilled laborers and experts monopolize
the jobs. Socialist schools must develop in the pupils a sense of self-
respect and initiative, and open to them a new horizon for ambition, not
helpless slaves for capitalistic regime. Against the foolish theory of the
six days' creation of the world, we must place the Darwin theory. The modern
school, supported by scientists of reputation is exactly what we want.

Capitalists should not rule the schools and make the system conform to their
selfish desire to promote intellectual ignorance.

SLOVENIAN

Proletarec, Vol. 11, No. 450, April 25, 1916.

MAY-DAY MANIFESTATION.

The Organizing Committee of the United Jugoslav Socialist Organizations in Chicago announced plans for a May-Day Manifestation, which will be held in co-operation with Bohemian organizations on May 1.

All organizations willing to participate in this manifestation should send their representatives to Bohemian Hall, "Spravedluost" at Loomis Street and Blue Island Avenue, from which place the parade will begin to move.

All organizations are urged to take part in the projected parade and to attend the mass-meetings following.

Proletarec, Vol. 10, No. 385, Jan. 26, 1915.

ANNUAL FINANCIAL REPORT FOR YEAR 1914.

JUGOSLAV SOCIALIST FEDERATION.

a) Received--$6,609.89
b) Paid------$6,407.11
   In treasury$ 203.78
c) Property--$3,366.00

I E

Proletarec, Vol. 5, No. 132, arch 22, 1910.

OBSERVANCE OF PARIS COMMUNE.   WPA (ILL) PPOJ 30275

The Slovenian Socialist Club No. 1 in Chicago organized a celebration in memory
of the Paris Commune. This celebration took place Sunday, March 20 in the Grand
Hall on Central Avenue.

The program was excellent. The Jugoslav Workers' Musical Band and Jugoslav Workers'
choir offered numerous songs and other musical selections.

SLOVENIAN

Proletareo, Vol. 4, No. 105, Sept. 14, 1909.

AIM OF THE SLOVENIAN SOCIALIST ORGANIZATION IN AMERICA

The principal aim of the Slovenian Socialist Organization in America is to organize all Slovenian workers into an International Socialist Party for the defense and interests of the working class, with no objection to religion or race; also to work on a wide distribution of workers' literature and newspapers; to organize public lectures, meetings, etc.; also to advocate and help our workers become citizens of this country and enjoy the full rights of citizens; and help members with moral and financial support in case of need.

<u>Proletarec</u>, Vol. 3, No. 26, March 10, 1908.

SLOVENIAN WOMEN'S SOCIALIST CLUB.

The Slovenian Women's Socialist Club, "Proletarka", has been organized in Chicago.

President: Berta Preshern
Secretary: Mary Grilec
Address: 674 W. 21st. Place, Chicago
Monthly meetings: third week in month.

Proletarec, Vol. 3, No. 18, Jan. 14, 1908.   WPA (ILL) PROJ 30275

FINANCIAL STATEMENT OF THE JUGOSLAV SOCIALIST FEDERATION
FROM JUNE 20, TO DEC. 1, 1907.

Balance from June 20, 1907 - - $8.55

Receipts

Advertisement in <u>Proletarec</u> - $122.15
Fees - - - - - - - - - - - -   51.22
Donations - - - - - - - - - -   6.30
Miscellaneous Receipts - - -   3.46
From Sales of Literature   2.00
                     Total - $193.68

Paid Out

Office Expenses - - - - - - $ 14.57
Commissions - - - - - - - - -   9.00
Printing - - - - - - - - - -   105.00
Refund - - - - - - - - - - -   26.15
Management - - - - - - - - -   1.75
Shares of Printing Shop - - -   24.11
                     Total - $180.58

Fr. Podlipec, Pres.   Cash on Hand - - - - $13.10   John Petrich, Treas.

Proletarec, Vol. 3, No. 18, Jan. 14, 1908.   WPA (ILL) PROJ 30275

JUGOSLAV SOCIALIST FEDERATION.

The Jugoslav Socialist Club No. 1 has been established in Chicago. Its headquarter's
are at:

        Owner of the Premises: Fr. Mladieh
                          387 S. Center Avenue, Chicago
        President: Anton Preshern
        Secretary: Frank Podlipec

Meetings will be held on the last Saturday of every month.

BY-LAWS OF THE SLOVENIAN SOCIALIST FEDERATION IN AMERICA

At its last meeting, the Slovenian Socialist Club, in Chicago, drew up
the by-laws and regulations for the Slovenian Socialist Federation in
America, and asked that these by-laws be published in Proletarec for
the purpose of public acceptance. All comments pertaining to any
changes must be sent to Mr. Anton Preshern.

The Slovenian Socialistic Federation in America is the propagator of
the socialist program of the Socialist Party in America.

                                MEMBERSHIP

Every person, male or female, of Slovenian descent, who is 18 years of
age, and who recognizes the socialist teachings, will be gladly accepted
as a member of this Federation. All members, active or inactive, of any
socialist lodge in America automatically become members of this Federation and may exercise their rights to vote.

Proletarec, February 1906.

PURPOSES

The main purpose of this Federation is to spread socialist propaganda either in writing or in speech, and to spread socialist doctrines in America and Jugoslavia.

In order to fulfill these purposes, the Federation will organize lectures, and will print books, leaflets, pamphlets, newspapers, etc.

BOARD OF DIRECTORS

All affairs of the Federation will be supervised by the board of directors, which will consist of three branches: administration, editorial and controller.

The administration branch will be supervised by six members: president, vice-president, financial secretary, editorial secretary, archive secretary and his assistant. The editorial branch, as well as the controller branch will be supervised by three members.

I E   - 3 -   SLOVENIAN
II B 2 d (1)
III H   Proletarec, February 1906.

ELECTION

In December of each year the Federation will hold an election for a new board of supervisors. For this election our first secretary will send a printed ballot to all clubs in America. On distributed ballots, will be printed the names of candidates. Because each club has its own election rights it is permitted to elect its own candidate. In such an instance the name of the candidate printed on the ballot can be scratched out and the candidate desired by the club may be substituted.

The final decision in the election will depend on the majority of ballots received by the substituted candidate.

In case of a tie in votes, a new election will be ordered.

All ballots received after the month of December will be valid.

Any changes desired pertaining to the election regulations must be sent not later than the month of November.

FEDERATION PRESS

The official organ of the Slovenian Socialist Federation will be
<u>Proletarec.</u> The owner of this publication can be any member of the
Socialist Party in America or Jugoslavia, who belongs to some club.
The editorial management is obliged to print any announcement,
article, debate, etc., no matter what the critics say.

In exceptional cases the editor has the right to request a correspondent's
identification as a member of the club.

The treasurer of the Federation is requested to publish a financial
statement every fourth month in the official organ.

SOCIALIST CLUBS

In every town or city in America, where a substantial number of Socialists
live, they have the right to organize their own club and elect their
board of supervisors. Monthly reports of their doings will be accepted

and published by Proletarec. Every Socialist living in Jugoslavia can
be a member of any club in America, no matter what nationality this
club represents.

SOCIALIST COURT

In case of a misunderstanding, or a quarrel between members of the Club,
such affairs must be settled by the Club, or the Federation Honor Court.

Each court consists of five members. In case of a tie in voting the
president's ballot will be the deciding vote.

If any person in a case shows dissatisfaction with the court's decision,
he has a right to appeal to the Federation Court, whose decision will
be considered final.

SUPERVISORS' DUTIES

In case the board of supervisors shows lack of interest in fulfilling

Proletarec, February 1906.

their duty, five members of the Federation can submit their complaint
to the secretary-treasurer, who will ask the entire membership for its
opinion by a vote of trust. In such cases the board of supervisors will
be suspended from their offices until the members' opinion is crystalized.

In case of the resignation of any member of the board of supervisors, the
secretary will announce new elections.

HEADQUARTERS OF THE FEDERATION

The official headquarters of the Slovenian Socialist Federation is in
Chicago, Illinois.

I. ATTITUDES
   F. Politics
      2. Part Played by Social and
         Political Societies

Proletarec, Vol. 13, No. 548, March 12, 1918.

SLOVENIAN REPUBLICAN ORGANIZATION IN
CHICAGO.

In regard to the resolution, which was accepted at a recent meeting of the Republican organization and sent to several prominent leaders in Washington, we received th
following comments:

United States Senate,
Committee on Expenditures in the Department of State
February 5, 1918.

Mr. Charles Vosel, Chairman
Mr. Frank Zaitz, Secretary C. R. Z.
Chicago, Ill.

Gentlemen:

I am **very** much obliged to you for your communication of recent date, and I assure
you that the views of your organization will have my most sincere consideration.
                          Very Respectfully, Jas. Hamilton Lewis.

Proletarec, Vol. 13, No. 548, March 12, 1918.

2) Department of Justice,
   Washington, D. C.

Frank Zaitz, Esq.
Secretary of Local Organization S. R. Z.
Chicago, Ill.

Sir:

The department is in receipt of a copy of the resolution adopted by the Slovenian Republican Alliance at a mass meeting held at Pulaski Hall on January 27, 1918, and thanks for transmitting the same.

                              Respectfully,
                              Charles Waren,
                              Ass't. Attorney General
                              For: The Attorney General

Proleterec, Vol. 13, No. 340, Jan. 15, 1913.

CONCERT.

Slovenian Republican Organization in Chicago is setting the stage for a concert and dance, to be held at 1709-15 S. Ashland Avenue, near 18th street, Jan. 27.

The program for entertainment is varied and interesting, and we hope that our Slovenian people in Chicago and vicinity, who sympathize with Republican ideals, will be present. Slovenians must show their solidarity in fight for social and economic order in this land.

Interest in the Republican Organization and its future is established by the fact, that in a very short time after the Republican Organization opened a branch in Chicago, we had over 800 members, with practically all Slovenian societies participating in the work of soliciting members. We are proud to announce the fact that fifteen Slovenian societies have signed for membership of the Republican organization.

Proletarec, Vol. XII, No. 537, Dec. 25, 1917.

SLOVENIAN REPUBLICAN ORGANIZATION.

Executive Board:
Frank Bostich, Filip Godina, Martin Konda, Etlin Kristan, Frank Kerze, Anton
Terlovec, Jose Zavortnik.

Control Committee:
Matt. Petrovich, Ludvik Benedik, Frank Verancich.

Central Committee:
John Ermec, Ivan A. Kaker, Ivan Kuzar, Anton Motz, Frank Mravlija, and others.

Interest in Slovenian Republican Organization in America is growing so rapidly,
that members of this party in Chicago, found it necessary to appoint our people
here with the aim of this organization, and decided therefore to organize a mass-
meeting on January 1, 1917 at 3 P.M. on the premises of "Prosveta."

I. ATTITUDES
F. Politics
6. Graft and
Corruption

Proletarec, Vol. 10, No. 409, July 13, 1915.

WHERE IS $60,000?

After receipt of the warrant for the arrest of M. Sullivan issued by Judge Horner, the sheriff's office went on the trail of the former Clerk of the Probate Court in Chicago.

The sheriff is anxious to ask M. Sullivan a few questions concerning the disappearance of just $60,000 from the fund for orphaned children.

Mr. Sullivan has been Clerk of this Court for the past seventeen years, and the shortage was discovered recently, after the accounts had been audited.

Mr. Sullivan was given a considerable length of time to cover the shortage, but failed to do so and the warrant was sworn for his imprisonment; but all efforts to find him have failed and so the $60,000 is gone.

I. ATTITUDES
   G. War

Proletarec, Vol. 13, No. 576, Sept. 24, 1918.

LIBERTY BONDS AND SLOVENES IN CHICAGO.

All Slovenian societies located and active in Chicago had a meeting, which took place on September 21, 1918 at the hall, "Little Bohemia". The purpose of this meeting was to organize subscriptions for "Liberty Bonds".

The following societies were represented by their delegates:
1) Women's Society 78
2) Society: "Neze"
3) Singing Society "Lira"
4) Newspaper "Proletarec"
5) Society: "Slovenski Dom"
6) Society: "Fr. Fekker"
7) Society: "Slavia"
8) Society #17
9) Newspaper: Cas
10) Newspaper: Prosveta
11) Society: "Lincoln"
12) Society: "Jugoslavia"
13) Society: "Danica"

Proletarec, Vol. 13, No. 576, Sept. 24, 1918. WPA (ILL) PROJ 3527E

14) Society: "St. Stefan"
15) Society #100
16) Society: "St. Deuzina"
17) Slovenian Worker's Sokol
18) Society: "St. Juraj"
19) Society: "Narodin Vitezi"
20) Society: "Woodrow Wilson"

This meeting showed the excellent spirit of Slovenian people and their hearty interest for the welfare of their new fatherland, America.

II. CONTRIBUTIONS
   AND ACTIVITIES
   A. Vocational
      2. Industrial and Commercial

Majski Glas (May Herald), May 1937.

THE FUTURE OF BUILDING AND LOAN ASSOCIATIONS
By Donald J. Lotrich

For a good many years Building and Loan Associations have enjoyed the
confidence and good will of our people and have therefore played quite
prominently in their lives. Particularly has that been true in localities where our people have settled more compactly and in larger numbers.
Say what we will, these institutions have been used and are still being
used by the progressive and thrifty elements as savings institutions.
Many, many have used to advantage the credit and services of these
institutions to acquire their homes. Some who were not so prudent or
who overestimated their earning ability and plunged too deeply into
debt, however, could not be rescued even by such institutions. Wherever
the management was wise and alert to the trends and conditions it can
be generally said that there the association was a great asset to the
people and to the community. The direct opposite is true wherever the
management ignored the principal factors of good business management
and economic tendencies.

The mere fact that we were able to survive the depression gives us

Majski Glas (May Herald), May 1937.

assurance and courage to continue. But I know that mere words are
insufficient to assure anyone anything in the present capitalistic
set-up. It's got to be more than that. Action must accompany words.

Permit me to say, then, that the 1937 Board of Directors of the Jugoslav Building and Loan Association have adopted, among other things,
a goal of 160 new subscribers for 1937.

Ten have already begun to pay their weekly allotments. Twenty two more
have pledged to do the same in a short time. We are intent on disposing
of the real estate on hand and pay off the old obligations just as soon
as conditions warrant.

Incidentally, I might say that there is a brisk demand for homes and
that one property has already been sold and that a number of bids on
other properties have been received.

There can be no doubt but that the experiment of the Federal Government

Najski Glas (May Herald), May 1937.

in providing mortgage credit through Associations like ours has proved
successful. Hence, there can be no doubt but that greater support and
a more definite desire to participate in the work of these Associations
will be the continued policy of the Federal institution.

A nation's basic wealth is its land and homes and mineral deposits.

With a well organized mortgage reserve system behind it, there is no
sounder investment than the home mortgage cooperative units or mutual
associations give to the investor the maximum in returns. With management, foresight and vision there is every reason to believe that our
associations can still grow and prosper and give that service, both
to investor and borrower, that was given in the past.

Amerikanski Slovenec, Vol. XXXIV, No. 95, June 18, 1925

CONFERENCE OF THE CATHOLIC PRINTING SOCIETY EDINOST

On the 15th of June the Catholic Printing Society "Edinost" held its regular conference of priests and shareholders of this society, from Chicago and vicinity.

Rev. James Cerne, assisted by other priests, gave his blessing to the new printing machinery and the premises occupied by the printing shop.

After the blessing a banquet was given in honor of the guests and employees of this shop. The premises had been decorated for this occasion. After supper the president of the society, Mr. John Jerich, opened the program of music and songs. Among the speakers we noticed a number of guests from Ohio, Wisconsin and Illinois. All speakers pointed out the great need of a Catholic press, and expressed the opinion that only through this press will the American Slovenes be successful in the political and religious fields.

Amerikanski Slovenec, Vol. XXIV, No. 95, June 18, 1925

A comical interpretation of stories from Rev. Cerne's colorful life brought much laughter. The speakers selected as their keynote the idea of propaganda for an educational campaign. All suggestions were accepted by the audience with applause.

On this occasion we had the pleasure of hearing the brilliant voice of our well known singer, Miss Kosmach, who gave an artistic touch to this meeting.

In God we trust, and with His blessing upon our education work we strongly believe in our ability to carry on our national ideals with success, and gain dutiful recognition for our people here and abroad. Support, sympathy and recognition will be the best. testimony that our ideals are accepted and are bringing happiness to our people.

We rightfully call our society "Edinost," which means "unity", and it means also that we must strive to preserve this unity if we expect success and victory in our fight for existence as a Slovene nation. Such a noble goal as the preservation of national ideals is worth all the suffering, struggle and sacrifice in the world.

Please do not refuse your support to our society, and the society will do its share in building our national unity.

II. CONTRIBUTIONS
   AND ACTIVITIES
   B. Avocational and Intellectual
      1. Aesthetic
         a. Music

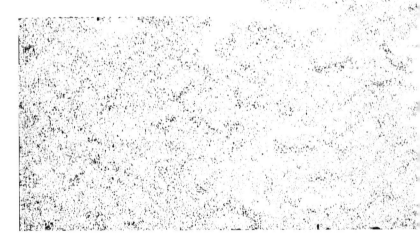

Memorial Book of the First all-
Slavic Singing Festival, 1934.

THE LIRA SLOVENE SINGING SOCIETY

In the year 1916 the Lira Singing Society was organized on the West Side of
Chicago, in the Slovene community which has its center at Cermak Road and
Lincoln Street, as the Tamburica Society, taking its name from the popular
Jugo-Slav instrument. The organizers were William Prijatel and John Weble.
The club grew so rapidly that in a very short time it had eighty members.
At that time it had a number of sponsoring members, and so it was decided
that it was strong enough to add a singing group to the original instrumen-
tal group. The name of the club was changed, and it became the Lira Sloven-
ian Singing and Tamburica Society.

Its object was to promote Slovene singing and Slovene instrumental music.
The following persons were its officers at the time of its organization:
John Weble, president, Adolph Misja, secretary, and Jack Juha, treasurer.

The singing group was under the direction of Mr. Juha, while Mr. Weble di-
rected the tamburica-players. At this time both divisions advanced steadily, and the concerts which they gave were successful because the Lira was
then the only Slovene singing and tamburica society in Chicago.

Since the World War had taken many of its members, the organization dropped
the tamburica division and continued as a singing society only. At present
the Lira Society has twenty active members, including three who have been
with the organization since the beginning, namely, Mrs. Lollie Nemanich,
Mr. John Weble, and Mr. Frank Kordesh. The Society for the last six years
has been without the financial aid of any sponsoring members and continues
to maintain itself by giving concerts once or twice a year. In its reper-
toire are selections from various operas and operettas, such as Martha, The
Minuet, Il Trovatore, and Madame Butterfly, and also many artistic Slovene
songs which had never before been introduced in Chicago.

The fifteenth anniversary of the founding of the Lira Society was celebrated on Sunday, April 3, 1932, by a concert in which some other Jugo-Slav
singing societies participated, among them two Slovene organizations, the
Adrija and the Preseren, and one Croatian club, the Croatia. On various
other occasions the Lira has cooperated with other Slavic singing societies.

In the period of its existence the Lira Singing Society has had the following directors: Mr. Jack Muha, Mr. Arno M. Hoss, Mr. Zindl, Mr. F. Kvederas,
and Mr. Gabriel Chrzanowski, who has been our instructor since 1926.

Memorial Book, 1934.

The officers at present are John Neble, president, Frank Kordesh, vice-president, Evelyn Fabian, secretary, Vera Kordesh, recording secretary, and Lollie Nemanich, treasurer.

Memorial Book of the First All-
Slavic Singing Festival, 1934.

THE ADRIJA SLOVENE SINGING SOCIETY

The name Adrija means Adriatic. The sky-blue Adriatic Sea has always been an object of tender affection and almost devout reverence for Slovenes, and their love for it is reflected in their songs. They share this feeling with their southern neighbors and kinsmen, the Croats. A number of Slovene and Croatian singing societies call themselves Adrija or Jadran.

The Adrija Slovene Singing Society of Chicago is a mixed choir. Since its organization fourteen years ago the number of its members has fluctuated. There have never been less than twenty-five nor more than forty-five active singers.

The Adrija choir is affiliated with the Slovene Roman Catholic Church of St. Stephen, at Twenty-second Place and Lincoln Street in Chicago. Besides its liturgical singing in the aforesaid church the society gives one or two concerts every year in the school hall adjacent to St. Stephen's Church,

and it often renders programs for the lodges, clubs, and fraternities of the
local community. It has also appeared on the concert programs of other Slovene singing societies in Chicago, namely, the Lira, the Zarja, the Sava,
and the Preseren, and at present it is cooperating with the oldest and largest of them all, the Slovan. Adrija was the first Slovene choir in Chicago
to attempt the radio field; it has appeared in four Slovene radio programs
over Station WHFC and in one program over Station WCFL. A number of Slovene
phonograph records are also included in its list of accomplishments. These
latter are characteristic sketches with dialogue and song, such as the Slovene Wedding Festival, the Announcement of Spring (Advent of St. George),
and others.

The Adrija choir by its untiring efforts and commendable sacrifices was instrumental in securing a new electro-pheumatic two-manual organ for St.
Stephen's Church, installed February 19, 1922.

The proceeds of the choir's various activities are turned over to the parochial treasury, and its needs are provided for, and its expenses paid by the
parish.

Memorial Book, 1934.

New members for the Adrija choir are constantly being recruited from the ranks of the local parochial grammar-school graduates.

The director of the Adrija Singing Society is Mr. Ivan Racic, organist of St. Stephen's Church. His connection with the choir goes back practically to its inception. Mr. Racic received some of his musical training in Europe and is now working for a degree in music at De Paul University in Chicago. He was the unanimous choice for leader of the Slovene aggregation of singers at the First All-Slavic Singing Festival in Chicago.

II B 1 a
II B 1 c (3)
II B 1 c (1)
II D 1
II D 2
V A 1
III G
I A 1 a
I D 1 b
I B 4
I G
I C
IV

Memorial Book

of First All - Slavic Singing Festival, 1934.

SLOVAN SINGING SOCIETY

Slovenes, like other Slavic nations, love and admire good music, vocal and instrumental. They love to sing on every occasion - at picnics, parties, dances, wedd-
ings, and christenings. This racial characteristic was the potential reason for
the organization of the Slovan Singing Society twenty-nine years ago(1905) in
South Chicago. Immigration to the United States was not restricted at that time,
and thousands of young men and women from the former Austrian provinces of Carniola,
Carinthia, and Lower Styria -all three included in Slovenia - crossed the Atlantic
in the hope of earning a better living under Uncle Sam than under the Austrian
double eagle. The group settling in South Chicago and the near-by Pullman district
lost no time in organizing their fraternal lodges, for America, unlike Europe,
did not provide government insurance against loss by sickness or injury. They
also united to establish singing clubs in the early nineties.

Memorial Book

of First All - Slavic Singing Festival, 1934.

The Slovan Society was the first Slovene club organized with a single object - the preservation of Slovene song in Chicago. This purpose is still the only motive that keeps the society in existence as years with their achievements roll by. At present the Slovan is the oldest Slovene singing society in the United States; like other societies and clubs, it has had difficulties throughout its long career. Financial problems, lack of proper instructors, the World War, emigration and immigration restrictions were some of the obstacles which at times almost ruined the organization. At present the Slovan has seventy active members, the majority of them men. Never before in its history has the Society had so large a membership.

Throughout its twenty-nine years of existence the Slovan Society has regularly given one or more concerts a year; sometimes as a male chorus, sometimes as a mixed chorus, and as a male chorus at times including both choruses in its program. In former years dramatic performances also were presented. The Slovan has at all times maintained friendly relations with other Slovene singing societies, and on many occasions it has co-operated with Slovene, Croatian, Servian, and German clubs in giving concerts. The outstanding events in the Society's history were the gala concert performances on its twentieth and twenty-fifth anniversaries in 1925 and 1930.

Memorial Book

of First All - Slavic Singing Festival, 1934.

An elaborate singing festival is contemplated for the thirtieth anniversary in 1935. The Slovan is the only Slovene singing society on Chicago's greater South Side. Its present headquarters are in the Calumet Park field house. In the course of its existence the Slovan has had seven directors, and Mr. Mirko G. Kuhel, the present director, has wielded the baton for the last nine and a half years. Mr. Kuhel came to America fourteen years ago. He has been a student at St. Stanislaus' College in Slovenia; he attended high school here and completed two years of college work. He was then appointed to an executive position in one of the Slovene-American fraternal insurance corporations and since that time had very little leisure for other activities.

Mr. Kuhel devotes his spare hours to directing the Slovan chorus because of his love for Slovene song. Since he received his education on both continents, he is particularly well adapted to give instruction in Slovene music both to immigrants and to American-born members of the choir. The Society has co-operated heartily in the movement to organize the United Slavic choral Societies of Chicago, and sincerely hopes that a permanent association will be founded.

Amerikanski Slovenec, February 17, 1926.

CONCERT BY THE SINGING SOCIETY "ADRIA"

Last Sunday our young singing society "Adria" gave a very successful concert with dance. On this occasion we noticed that our people got more and
more interested in that kind of entertainment. Many times we have called
our public to support morally and financially our cultural institutions,
and this call goes especially for the support of the singing society
"Adria," which in the short period of its existence already brought joy
and happiness in the life of our colony.

Our sincere thanks to all leaders and members of this organization.

Proletarec, Feb. 21, 1911.

SLOVENIAN WORKERS' SINGING CHOIR OREL

Slovenes from Chicago and vicinity are cordially invited to a concert, to
be presented by our well-known Slovenian Workers' Singing Choir "Orel." It
will be given on February 25, in the People's Hall, at Central Avenue and
18th Street.

II. CONTRIBUTIONS ▬▬▬▬▬▬▬
    AND ACTIVITIES
    B. Avocational and Intellectual
       1. Aesthetic
          c. Theatrical
             (1) Drama

Novi Svijet, Vol. IV, No. 34, March 24, 1927.

TWO COMEDY PLAYS

The Dramatic Section, Club No. 1, of the Jugoslav Socialist Federation, is giving a play and social Sunday, March 27, in the C. S. P. S. Hall, 18th and May Street, Chicago.

They will present two plays: one in the Slovenian language, "Lokalna Zeljeznica," (Local Train), in three acts, followed by "The Family Exit," in English.

The show starts at 3 P. M. A dance follows.

II B 1 c (1)

SLOVENIAN

WPA (ILL.) PROJ. 30275

<u>Americanski Slovenec</u>, Vol. XXV, No. 220, Nov. 12, 1926.

NIGHT OF ENTERTAINMENT

November 14th is marked in memory of our people in Chicago as a night of excellent entertainment. Our society No. 16, D. S. D., gave a dramatic play, "Sin," with the well known cast from the Catholic Dramatic Club. Despite the very poor employment situation which prevails among our people, the premises were filled up to the last inch and tickets were practically all sold.

After the dramatic performance young and old joined in dancing, which continued up to the early hours of the morning.

Amerikanski Slovenec, Vol. XXXV, No. 96, May 18, 1926.

NEW SLOVENIAN CATHOLIC DRAMATIC CLUB

We say it is news! Our newly organized Slovenian Catholic Dramatic Club
gave us its first performance, and it was good! For a long time we did
not have such opportunity to enjoy our native plays and hear our songs
sung and we left the premises with a feeling that we spent a few delight-
ful hours in our dear old country.

This performance brought us so close together that even our deadly enemies forgot their bad feelings. We felt that we were brothers and belonged
to the same race and nation.

Amerikanski Slovenec, Vol. XXXV, No. 135, July 15, 1926.

CATHOLIC DRAMATIC CLUB IN CHICAGO

The last winter season in Chicago was very joyful. Concerts, carnivals, bazaars, and all kinds of entertainment took place.

The Catholic Dramatic Club of Chicago is especially showing great activity, and each time when some of our societies decide to hold a meeting or amuse the public, the Catholic Dramatic Club gladly accepts the invitation.

We are requested by the management of the above named club to inform our societies that in case any of them desire to select their own play, it will be played by club members under one condition: That the society send a request and the name of the play in written form to the secretary of the Catholic Dramatic Club, Mr. Ludurg Skaja, 2118 W. 21 st Pl.

Amerikanski Slovenec, Vol. XXIV, No. 138, July 15, 1923.

They also advise giving the club at least two weeks time in order to
rehearse the play and be ready for a performance. We have also informed
that the present staff of players is not (large) enough to cover some
of the plays and we, with all our hearts, recommend those of our young
girls and boys, who feel able to play, to enroll in the club immediately.
It really will be a pity for all of us if such a big colony as Chicago's,
with thousands of our people, would not be able to supply the necessary
number of players and (thus) handicap the activities of this most important organization.

II. CONTRIBUTIONS
   AND ACTIVITIES
      B. Avocational and Intellectual
         1. Aesthetic
            c. Theatrical
               (3) Festivals, Pageants,
Fairs and Expositions

III B
I E   Proletarec, Apr. 18, 1911.

LEAGUE OF SOCIALIST YOUTH BAZAAR

The League of Socialist Youth is arranging a bazaar to raise funds for
the support of the <u>Daily Socialist</u> newspaper. It will be held April
27, 28, 29, and 30, in Schweitzer Hall, at Clark and Kinzie Sts. Tickets
will cost fifteen cents.

II. CONTRIBUTIONS
AND ACTIVITIES
B. Avocational and Intellectual
2. Intellectual
a. Libraries

Proletarec, Vol. 7, No. 269, Nov. 5, 1912.

SLOVENIAN LIBRARY IN CHICAGO

The Slovenian Library in Chicago organized by the Socialist Club No. 1, has become more and more popular and can be considered as a public institution of high
value. The management of this library does not spare efforts nor money in order
to fill its shelves with books, magazines, periodicals, etc., printed in the
Slovenian language. The greatest part of this reading material is ordered from
Lubljana, Jugoslavia.

The library also has a large selection of books and periodicals printed in English
for those who know or want to learn English thoroughly. It is true that our
people help this institution, especially since we know that the fees are as low
as $.15 per month.

The library is open every evening from 7:30 to 9 P.M., and is located at 1830 S.
Center Street on the premises of the Croation Library.

II. CONTRIBUTIONS
AND ACTIVITIES
B. Avocational and Intellectual
2. Intellectual
d. Publications
(1) Newspapers

Amerikanski Slovenec, Sept. 10, 1925. , SLOVENE

/SLOVENIAN NEWSPAPERS/

The Slovenian people in America are represented by more newspapers in America than any other nationality, proportionally. We do not see any reason to describe the great influence and importance of this press, but will name these existing publications, daily or weekly. They are as follows:

(1) Amerikanski Slovenec, Catholic organ; (2) Ave Maria, Church organ; (3) Glasilo Kskj, Catholic people organ; (4) American Country, Independent; (5) Glas Naroda, Anti-religious; (6) Enakopravnost, Anti-Church and Socialist; (7) Cas, Anti-Church; (8) Prosveta, Organ of the Slovenian National Benefit Society; (9) Proletarec, Radical; (10) Me. List SNP, Prosveta branch of Youth organization; (11) Glas Svobode, Radical; (12) Delavska Slovenia, Workers' organ; (13) Nas Doni, Independent; (14) Nova Doba, Independent.

Amerikanski Slovenec, Vol. XXXIV, No. 88, June 5, 1925.

WE MUST SUPPORT OUR NEWSPAPER

We notice that our friends and supporters accepted with great satisfaction
the enlarged size of our newspaper. We are receiving daily thousands of
letters from all parts of this country, congratulating us on our efforts
to improve the reading matter and enlarge the size of our daily. This makes
us happy and gives us energy to continue such policy.

But in order to fulfill the already made promises to give our readers a
newspaper of high standard and quality, as well as to meet the growing
expenses incurred with newspaper expansion, we must have additional capital.
We are in great need of a new and modern printing machinery to speed up
work on a higher rate circulation. New appearance of the newspaper enlarged
size, increase in reading matter, all these require more capital which, we
are sorry to say, we are unable to secure from any other sources except
from the reading public. Our plan to secure additional capital is plain,

Amerikanski Slovenec, Vol. XXXIV, No. 88, June 5, 1925.

we figure that the increased expenses can be covered by securing from
700 to 800 new subscribers, and we are strongly appealing to our readers
and friends for this support.

We do not need go further with an explanation why our Slovenes need their
own and the only Catholic newspaper, nor what benefits they are getting
by reading its very interesting and highly educational pages. We hope that
such reasons already have been printed on many pages of this paper, but
the only opinion we do express is that it would not be nice of Slovenes
if, in this critical hour for our newspaper's existence, they will with-
draw their helping hand. We do not have other means to provide additional
capital, and we must assure you that without sufficient capital this paper
cannot be published in an enlarged form or have better reading material.

Now that we have laid down our problem, it is up to you, friends and
readers, to help us with solicitation of a few hundred new subscribers,
and if you succeed in this work we will keep our promises of going to
the limit.

Amerikanski Slovenec, Vol. XXXIV, No. 88, June 5, 1925.

All Catholic organizations are requested to organize their work on solicitation, and as soon as we have the required number of new subscribers
filled, our work on developing the newspaper will be fast.

Amerikanski Slovenec, Vol. XXXV, No. 17, Jan. 27, 1925.

35TH ANNIVERSARY OF THE FIRST SLOVENIAN NEWSPAPER IN AMERICA

This year, 1926, is the 35th anniversary of the first Slovenien newspaper in America. Our great joy is fully justified and we believe it will be shared by all our friends in America.

We know what help we all got from Amerikanski Slovenec during many years of its existence. Friendly advice, interesting news concerning our life here and the people in the old country, educational and religious guarding, moral, and in many cases, even financial help: all what we are supposed to expect from a native publication we got, and got plenty of it. There is no doubt in our mind that we could not live without our newspaper. Our newspaper is our history; its power cannot be easily overlooked. Ask our old pioneers and leaders, our successful business people; all will confess that Amerikanski Slovenec played an important part in their life's struggles, in fights towards accomplishment.

Our newspaper was the strong cement that united our divided opinion, our

Amerikanski Slovenec, Vol. XXXV, No. 17, Jan. 27, 1925.

ideal of native unity.

It is true that our newspaper fulfills the ideal of native apostles. Thirty-five years ago the voice of a small newspaper told to our people the first truth, that there is hope for all of us in America to become solid in our ideas, economically powerful and a highly organized and respected nationality. From the Atlantic to the Pacific this friendly voice announced great news.

For years and years Amerikanski Slovenec has filled its pages with stories illustrating our life and it will be the truth and nothing else if we claim that this newspaper is a living history of our people in this country.

Amerikanski Slovenec was established Sept. 3, 1891. The first issue of this newspaper was printed on Racine Avenue, Chicago. The first issue and the others which followed during six months were a thing looking paper of two small pages. Even in this size Amerikanski Slovenec could not exist very long on account of chronical lack of money. For non-payment of rent it was evicted from its printing shop and forced to move to the Northside of Chicago. The only way to save the paper was to find someone who would have enough

Amerikanski Slovenec, Vol. XXXV, No. 17, Jan. 27, 1925.

money to finance it until subscriptions could cover the overhead. This
solution was found in a deal which brought about the sale of Amerikanski
Slovenec to an ex-priest from Tower, Minn., Father Buh, who paid $600
for it. The man who started it and owned it is our Chicago Slovenian
Mr. Anton Murnik.

Success came very soon, not through the financial standing of Father Buh,
but through his hard work and influence. There never were enough subscribers to pay expenses, but Father Buh found the friendly support of
a few sympathizers. This fact is convincing that it is not money what
will keep a publication in existence, but the personal influence and
energy of its managers.

Amerikanski Slovenec moved to Tower, Minn., where Father Buh held a position
as pastor in St. Martin's Church.

The worst problem in the existence of this newspaper was lack of good
Slovenian writers. Reporters from small towns were not skilled in editorial
work. Translated articles sounded so funny in the Slovene language that

Amerikanski Slovenec, Vol. XXXV, No. 17, Jan. 27, 1925.

many readers complained that they could not understand clearly the meaning
of the articles.

At that time Amerikanski Slovenec had already 600 subscribers and more than
200 copies were distributed free of charge. In spite of that, financial
difficulties were pressing so hard that Father Buh was forced to sell it.
This time, it seems, luck was on the side of Amerikanski Slovenec. The
new owner, Tiskovna Druzba, Joliet, Ill., put the publication on a paying
basis, but its normal existence came to an end on account of the trans-
fer of its chief stockholder, Rev. Susterich, who went to Europe. Then
came the joke of a lifetime: the Slovenian newspaper passed into German
ownership. This period was fatal for the newspaper, but salvation came
again when Amerikanski Slovenec was bought by its present owner, Tiskovna
Druzba Edinost.

We must repeat again that for over 35 years our Amerikanski Slovenec has
been the beginning of everything in Slovenian life in America. We simply
cannot imagine the existence of our social, cultural and benevolent societies without Amerikanski Slovenec. We are proud of being owners of
our own and oldest newspaper, and intend to support it to the end.

Znanje, Vol. IV, No. 38, Dec. 24, 1921.

FOR SLOVENIAN WORKERS

We recommend to Slovenian workers the newspaper Delavska Slovenija (The
Working Slovenia), which is the property of the Jugoslav Cultural Club
of Milwaukee. The address is: Delavska Slovenija, 383 First Avenue,
Milwaukee, Wisconsin. Subscription $2.50 per year.

Today that is the only Slovenian paper in the hands of Slovenian workers,
which will represent the interests of the working class in the spirit of
our times.

We call on Croatian and Serbian workers to recommend said paper to Slovenian workers, wherever they meet them. With this paper Slovenians have
filled a gap which existed for a long time, not having a paper for
Slovenian workers.

SLOVENIAN

Proletarec, Vol. 8, No. 315, Sept. 23, 1913.

STATEMENT OF THE OWNERSHIP, MANAGEMENT, CIRCULATION, ETC. OF
PROLETAREC.

Published weekly in Chicago, Illinois. Statement required by the Act of August
24, 1914.

Editor: Frank Skof, 4006 W. 31st Street, Chicago, Ill.
Managing Editor: Fr. Skof, 4006 W. 31 st Street, Chicago, Ill.
Publisner: Jugoslovenska Delavska
        Jiskovna Druzba, 4006 W. 31st Street, Chicago, Ill.
Owner; Slovenian Section of So. Slavic Socailist Federation.
        Frank Podlipec, Trustee.

Proletarec, Vol. 4, No. 93, June 22, 1909.

RESOLUTION CONDEMNING GLAS SVOBODE

The Delegate Committee of the Socialist Party of Cook County, session held June 13, 1909, at 180 W. Washington St., Chicago, Ill., endorsed the following resolution:

To the Cook County Delegate Committee, Grievance Committee Report in the case of 10th and 11th Ward Branches of the South Slovenian organization vs. Glas Svobode.

The evidence submitted to the grievance committee is to the effect that the paper, Glas Svobode, is not a socialist paper.

Its manager and owner, Martin Konda, admitted that it is an independent and free thought advocate, and that he is not a member of the socialist party.

Now, therefore, as said Glas Svobode has been listed by other well established party organs, and also supported by and through party commendation, and in view of the above unquestioned evidence, we, the Grievance Committee, find that said paper is not a socialist paper in the sense that other papers of the Socialist Party are (although it has in the past shown an apparent friendship and support

Proletareo, Vol. 4, No. 93, June 22, 1909.

to the Socialist Party), we, therefore, recommend that the county secretary be
instructed to send a copy of this resolution to the national secretary of the
Socialist Party, who will submit it to the socialist press.

Fraternally submitted,

L. W. Hardy, J. W. Born, A. Fishman, A. A. Patterson, Jas. P. Larsen, Committee.

Indorsed and accepted by the Delegate Committee, Socialist Party of Cook County,
session held June 13, 1909.

G. T. Fraenckel, Sec'y.

Proletarec, Vol. 4, No. 93, June 22, 1909.

DISCRIMINATION AGAINST GLAS SVOBODE AND ITS OWNER

On Dec. 26, 1908, the Slovenian Socialistic Club No. 1 in Chicago, issued a
resolution condemning false representation by Glas Svobode and discriminating
against its owner, M. Konda.

The resolution reads as follows:- Whereas Glas Svobode, the so-called socialist
newspaper published at 597 W. 20th St., Chicago, Ill., in the Slovenian language
and owned by Martin Konda, proved itself through many articles, notes and para-
graphs - especially through a certain article published in its issue, No. 43,
dated Oct. 23, 1908, in which it recommended a Democratic candidate for election
as non-socialistic and treasonable to the socialist principles and platform, and
to the Socialist Party at large; whereas Glas Svobode admitted in issue No. 43
dated Oct. 23, 1908, frankly with the words: "We never said that Glas Svobode
would be a Socialist paper", as a non-socialistic action before the English
Socialist Party, unfamiliar with the language and character of the paper and
yet seeks financial aid from the Party; whereas, the said paper, Glas Svobode,
declared itself in issue No. 43 dated Oct. 23, 1908, as a free-thinking and progressive paper, but still tells its readers how good a friend it is to the working people, so that the workers will buy the paper and thereby help fill the

Proletareo, Vol. 4, No. 93, June 22, 1909.

pookets of its owner, Martin Konda.

Therefore, be it resolved by members of South Slovenian Socialist Branch, Tenth
Ward, Chicago, Cook County, Ill., at a regular meeting assembled Dec. 26, 1908,
that said Glas Svobode is no more worthy of any moral or financial support from
any existing socialist party or from socialists at large, and therefore is put
on the unfair list of all socialists and class-conscious workers; and be it
further

Resolved, that a copy of this resolution be sent to the Executive Committee of the
Cook County Socialist Party for adoption and to the national secretary of the
Socialist Party of the U. S. for distribution to every socialist paper or maga-
zine, to be given as wide a publication as possible.

Chicago, Ill., Dec. 26, 1908.

Chairman - Mike Kuloveo
Secretary - Frank Podlipeo

Proletareo, Vol. 1, No. 8, August, 1906.

TO ALL SLOVENE AND CROATIAN MEMBERS
OF THE SOCIALIST FEDERATION

The Executive Branch of the Socialist Party in Cook County, Illinois decided
to publish a resolution, as follows:

Slovenian Comrades, Attention!

Whereas, it has been made known to the County Central Committee of Cook County,
Ill., on complaint of the Slovenian comrades composing the South Slovanian
Branch No. 11, that the Glas Svobode, owned by one, M. V. Konda, and published
in this city (Chicago), is preaching openly against socialism in its columns,
and

Whereas, this paper was at one time used by the Slovenian comrades as their official organ, and on account of its open attacks on socialism, it has ceased to
be such, and

Whereas, the said M. V. Konda has been, but is not now, a member of the Socialist party, and

Proletareo, Vol. 1, No. 8, August, 1906.   WPA (ILL. PROJ 30275

Whereas, the Slovenian comrades have now a paper named Proletareo, owned col-
lectively by them, published in the city of Chicago, and printed in the Slovenian
and Croatian languages; be it therefore

Resolved, that we condemn the action of M. V. Konda and consider as unfair and
unjust his attacks against the Socialist movement and its noble aim in behalf of
oppressed and down-trodden humanity; and we, therefore, call upon all Slovenian
comrades to give to Proletareo their loyal and financial support; be in further

Resolved, that a copy of these resolutions be printed in the Chicago Socialist,
a copy transmitted to the national office, and also that we ask the socialist
press of America to publish same with a view to giving these resolutions as wide
publicity as possible.

     Published by order of Cook County Central Committee.

II B 2 d (1)   SLOVENIAN
I E

Proletarec, Vol. 1, No. 1, Jan. 1906.

                                                             W A RA VILL : PROJ. 30275

EDITOR'S NOTICE.

With this first issue of the Proletarec, Slovenes of the working class came into
the intellectual world with their own publication. This step toward mass organization can be considered a real accomplishment of the working class, which never
has the opportunity to express its socialistic opinion.

Until today Slovene workers did not own or publish their own newspaper; therefore
it was impossible to openly state their opinion. All existing Slovene newspapers
were owned and published by people who were against the workers' interests. With
the aid of the Proletarec we hope that workers will understand that this publication is the only powerful and sincere means of gaining knowledge of our social,
economic, and religious statute, as well as to learn the whole truth that the
capitalists are the most dangerous enemies of the working class.

Proletarec' pages will always be wide open to workers for criticism. Workers need
not be afraid that their correspondence or articles will be thrown into the waste-
basket, because their contents are not favorable to the capitalistically inclined

Proletarec, Vol. 1, No. 1, Jan. 1906.   WPA (ILL.) PROJ 30275

newspaper owners.

Proletarec will offer select and rich reading material, which will consist of:
extracts from American newspapers, magazines, etc.; humorous stories; economic
and social references; and the strict policy of defending working class interests.
It will keep workers posted and well informed about international and local hap-
penings and will depict our socialistic fight for workers' rights.

For the time being the Proletarec will be issued only once a month and will be
printed on eight pages. Subscriptions will be only fifty cents for one year,
remittance to be sent to the address of our comrade, Anton Peshern, 678 W. 17th
Street, Chicago, Ill.

Articles and all correspondence should be addressed to 483 Loomis Street, Chicago,
Illinois.

Signed:
Andrey Popravne, President.

2. Intellectual
   g. Forums, Discus
      and Lectures

Proletarec, Jan. 2, 1917.

LECTURE ON SOCIALISM

·The Jugoslav Socialist Club No. 1 in Chicago has shown its educational
activity during the winter of this year by organizing a few very interesting
lectures, one of which is on the subject, "Socialism". This lecture proved
how little our people know about Socialism, and how badly they need to be
educated in Social Science.

II B 2 f
I E

SLCVENIAN

Proleturec, Vol. 7, No. 486, Jan. 2, 1917.

WPA (ILL) PROJ 30275

LECTURE ON SOCIALISM.

The Jugoslav Socialist Club No. 1 in Chicago has shown its educational activity during the winter of this year, by organizing a few very interesting lectures, one of which is on the subject, "Socialism". This lecture proved how little our people know about Socialism, and how badly they need to be educated in social science.

II. CONTRIBUTIONS
   AND ACTIVITIES
   D. Benevolent & Protective
      Institutions
      1. Benevolent Societies

Majskiglas, (The May Herald), Vol. XVLL, May 1937.

IN THE VANGUARD

Progressive Slovene Fraternal Benefit Societies in this country today among
which the Slovene National Benefit Society is the largest,are the work of
pioneer Socialists, who had foresight, men who realized that the workers
are left to shift for themselves and are exploited on every hand unless they
are strongly organized. Therefore, the Socialists were pioneering the ground
for the unions, for the cooperative movement, for educational work and at the
same time were fighting for old age pensions and other types of social insurance.

That was the work they were doing thirty years ago. At that time private
insurance companies were the only type of insurance companies in the field.
Socialists realized at that time that private insurance companies were in the
field to reap as much profit for their owners as possible. Today it is well
known that they are a legalized racket.

To the Jugoslav Socialist Federation and its official publication, Proletarec,

Majskiglas, (The May Herald), Vol. XVLL, May 1937.

we owe a debt of gratitude for the noble work it has been carrying on among
the old generation of Slovenes in America and the American-born Slovenes
for over three decades in the political, economic and industrial fields.

II D 1   SLOVENIAN
II D 2
I E
        Majskiglas, (The May Herald), Vol. XVII, May 1937. WPA (ILL) PROJ. 3027.

IN THE VANGUARD

Progressive Slovene Fraternal benefit Societies in this country today,
among which the Slovene National Benefit Society is the largest, are the
work of pioneer Socialists, who had foresight, men who realized that
the workers are left to shift for themselves and are exploited on every
hand unless they are strongly organized. Therefore the Socialists were
pioneering the ground for the unions, for the cooperative movement,
for educational work and at the same time were fighting for old age
pensions and other types of social insurance.

That was the work they were doing thirty years ago. At that time private insurance companies were the only type of insurance companies in
the field. Socialists realized at that time that private insurance
companies were in the field to reap as much profits for their owners
as possible. Today it is well known that they are a legalized racket.

II D 1   - 2 -   SLOVENIAN
II D 2
I E   Majskiglas, Vol. XVII, May 1937.   WPA (ILL.) PROJ 30275

To the Jugoslav Socialist Federation and its official publication, Pro-
letaroc, we owe a debt of gratitude for the noble work it has been
carrying on among the old generation of Slovenes in America and the
American-born Slovenes for over three decades in the political, economic and industrial fields.

SLOVENIAN

WPA (ILL.) PROJ 3027?

Amerikanski Slovenec, Vol. XXXVII, No. 227, Nov. 27, 1928.

AMALGAMATION OF CHICAGO K. S. K. LODGES

It had long been the desire of our people in Chicago that all small organizations, the existence of which, it seems, always have been endangered by
lack of members and financial conditions, to be united in one strong
society. It took a long time to come to actual amalgamation, but at last
it was accomplished to the satisfaction of all.

We, Slovenians in Chicago, had over fifteen small benevolent lodges. Upkeep
of such number of lodges with members of same nationality, with similar
rules and regulations, looks just foolish. People wasted money on so many
rents, secretaries, etc., and if we are to take into consideration personal
jealousy among officials of those small lodges, here we have a clear picture
of the handicap which holds the activities down.

No wonder that a great number of members of various lodges started protest-
ing against such doings, and after quite a fierce fight, they succeeded
in bringing unification and amalgamation.

Amerikanski Slovenec, Vol. XXXVII, No. 227, Nov. 27, 1928.

The new society was named United Lodges of Chicago K. S. K. Jednote. The
general idea of this new united organization is as follows: To keep the
organization's expenses down as much as possible; to increase sick benefit
for outstanding members; strong representation on national conventions;
promotion of good will among former members of small lodges; stronger support of our church St. Stjefan, etc.

We all must admit the great importance of such unity and are sincerely
congratulating the individuals on the hard work which brought this excellent idea to life.

II D 1
II B 2 d (1)
II B 2 d (2)   SLOVENIAN
III A   Proletarec, Vol. XXII, No. 1024, May Day 1927.
III E
II B 3   YOUTH IN THE SLOVENE FRATERNAL SOCIETIES

New thoughts and ideas develop every day. These new thoughts and
ideas must find new outlets in the same manner as any mechanical
implement or device. New implements, new thoughts and ideas are rarely
accepted unanimously, and until they are accepted, they must struggle
for their existence.

The young generation in the Slovene National Benefit Society has
developed new conceptions. To put these into operation under the
old system would be impossible, so nothing more desirable could have
happened than to have them branch into separate lodges in accordance
with their new ideas.

These new thoughts could not possibly be of any value to the parent
lodges; yet when they were properly assembled in their new forms
and put into operation, they met with surprising success. Unheard

Proletarec, Vol. XXII, No. 1024, May Day 1927.

of events, houses filled to capacity, things done just a little
different from the others. From the way these events were received,
we must feel that they were welcome wholeheartedly. It is our
desire and our purpose to keep building the fraternal spirit and
to keep pace with the most up-to-date styles of entertainment.

But even today, after proving unusually successful (functioning for
over a year and a half) some people still question the right of
young English-speaking Slovenes to organize into subordinate lodges.
Nevertheless, we must say that a big majority of the membership,
as well as the main body of officials, have given the movement
considerable support. In the main, however, it is not our purpose
nor is it proper for any participant or sympathizer to denounce
those not actually in favor of the movement, but rather to produce
evidence and proof to convince them that the policies pursued are
safe, sound, and justifiable. All claims that the young generation
could not exist and function should be banished immediately, for

SLOVENIAN

Proletarec, Vol. XXII, No. 1024, May Day 1927.

the performances of the past year well verify our statement that
more life and energy in the subordinate lodges has never been
brought to light. Of course, reference is made to the seventeen
English-speaking lodges of the SNPJ. Baseball and other sports
did not materialize as many predicted. Instead, membership cam-
paigns, dances, picnics, and other means of obtaining funds to
bolster the locals were instituted. One could venture to say that
these newly organized people are considerably more interested in
the affairs of their respective lodges than can be said of the
majority of the elders.

We don't doubt a bit that it was likewise with our parent lodges.
Good will, plenty of life and enthusiasm, and mainly excellent
results were obtainable when they were founded. But goodness how
this has diminished! Solely for the reason that the discussions
and thoughts concurred in were of the plain repeated style. What
we propose to do, however, is to use variety, by giving the young
generation the most modern disposition and meanin_ of fraternal ism;

Proletarec, Vol. XXII, No. 1024, May Day 1927.

the most up-to-date kind of amusement and entertainment; and the most
sincere cooperation and friendship.

Experience is the best instructor. And while a few profess to have
an exceptionally rare collection of knowledge, the membership is
learning from day to day; correcting the inaccuracies of previous
mornings. As time passes, a better system will be instituted as
the result of a better understanding of the fraternal situation.
As a general rule most of the young element is fairly well situated
in other English fraternal organizations, so that our task of
interesting them is somewhat difficult. Other fraternal organizations
have more to offer in the way of recreation than the SNPJ. Consequently the above is true. Organizers must use precaution and good
judgment, because the disposition of those of the age limit is very
indefinite and quite obscure. We must not only talk fraternalism
to them; no, that will never do. It is essential that we mention
social functions as well, until they have sufficiently mastered

SLOVENIAN

Proletarec, Vol. XXII, No. 1024, May Day 1927.

the scope of our field. You elders - your tasks were hard. Ours are
none the easier. Lend us your support; especially in the localities
where the population is widely scattered. The future of any Slovene
fraternal organization lies in the hands of the offspring. Similar
expressions are heard and read frequently. But it is not sufficient
to merely speak and write these words. It is necessary that these
remarks be backed with moral and financial support. And what about
the Slovene language? What effect will these new organizations
have upon it? Heated discussions on the subject are witnessed
regularly. From the most timid tales to the most capable defensive
arguments one is able to pick statements that would astonish even
the most unconcerned bystander. Some fear that the Slovene fraternal
organizations have reached their limit; that the English subsidiary
is their only salvation. Others quite differently proclaim no fear
for the language, even for the distant future. And so we conceive
the opinion that no immediate change is to take place in our
generation because within the rank and file there exist a large

percentage of those favorable to the organization of these English
lodges yet willing to sacrifice time and money for the development
of the Slovene language.

It is true that the official business of these lodges is transacted
in the English language, but it is also true that a greater percentage
of these youngsters attempt to either speak, read, write, or sing
in the Slovene language now more than heretofore. Prosveta is read
with delight, for it is convenient to glance from its pages to the
other sections for various announcements and suggestions. What is
more, magazines such as Mladinski List and Proletarec, while not
in the limelight, bear great watching. Perfected to a higher degree
of satisfaction, such magazines will be of great assistance in
partially keeping up the nationality. However, if the Slovene language is destined to extinction in this country, the English-speaking
lodges will not be the cause nor will such lodges bear the responsibility. Besides being a well-balanced fraternal organization, the
Slovene National Benefit Society is known to be a powerful weapon

Proletarec, Vol. XXII, No. 1024, May Day 1927.

when used in defense of the workers.

Without question it must be said that conditions, both working and living, have been improved. Organizations such as our fraternal order have been responsible, at least in part, in bringing about such improvement. You might consider such action as entering politics, but politics or otherwise, if the steps taken will bring about better living and working conditions, I deem it essential and necessary to say that our fraternal societies continue pursuing such tactics as long as the prevailing system of plundering the masses last. The Jugoslav Socialist Federation and its educational department is another institution which is also active in all such struggles, as is the League for Industrial Democracy. Knowing this, how can we fail to support them? Remembering that the years will tell the story of your present behavior, let us make history as it has never been made before.

In conclusion it is necessary to appeal to the Jugoslavs of this

SLOVENIAN

Proletarec, Vol. XXII, No. 1024, May Day 1927.

country to help build up their race by organizing new English-speaking
lodges, to keep and uphold the race by bringing up their offspring
so they can speak the Jugoslav language and to support such institutions from whom most benefit is derived. If you do this, we can
assure you that our language will not die; that the movement will
grow and prosper and will not astonish or amaze anyone.

Donald J. Lotrich.

SLOVENIAN

Proletarec, Vol. 22, No. 1024, May-Day Issue, 1927.

THE PIONEERS - THEIR POSSIBILITIES

It has been said quite often that Pioneer Lodge No. 559, S.N.P.J., (Slovenia
National Benefit Society) originated Nov. 13, 1925. The charter bears the in-
scription of twenty young men and women who gathered on that day to plant the
seed which has flourished and blossomed into success in the field of activities
and membership.

Nature has planted us amidst a pleasing environment and atmosphere, in which we
have found sparkling life and social activities aplenty. Good will and content-
ment has reigned with us always, and what we did not inherit we procured for ourselves.

The whole wide world should know that the Pioneers were the first English speaking fraternal lodge of any Jugoslav fraternal society in the world. Is this
boasting? Well, not exactly; but we wish to bring out the importance and significance of - "the first in the entire world". That phrase has probably more
meaning than any consideration you have ever given it. Have not the Pioneers
reason to feel proud? We can safely say that our relations with the parent organization have always been most respectful, and as we have often said, it is
their existence and their comfort which has necessitated such actions as we have
undertaken. A bright and unsurpassed future can be visualized. We can see the
Pioneer Lodge of 1942, the largest of any lodge under the fold of the Slovenska

Narodna Potporna Jednota. Its membership must reach one thousand. Do you know
why this is possible? Because we have adopted a broadminded program which will
reach everyone; because of our willingness to cooperate to the fullest extent;
and because we have the spirit and the knowledge of our power. We shall carry
on until we reach our goal.

We all realize the importance of the struggle, likewise its handicaps; but by
turning every opportunity into a reality and favoring those who labor to make
our very existence easier, we shall eventually surpass our prediction.

Amerikanski Slovenec, Vol. XXXV, No. 111, June 9, 1926.

THE RICHEST SLOVENIAN BENEVOLENT SOCIETY

The best answer we can offer to Slovenian National Benefit Society with regard to the accusation that our organization is progressing slowly, is the recent statistic. Our organization, as it can be found in the last financial report, has a capital of $1,535,000, which divided on 30,000 widow members that are being cared for by our society, will give a sum of $51.16 to each member, as benefit. Now, the official organ of SNPJ, in its last report shows that the benefit for a member amounts to only $42.46

Another part in SNPJ's financial report shows that the organization's capitalization is valued $42.46 per member, whereas our valuation shows $51.16 per member.

With this information we are offering to the people of the Slovenian nation the right way to find out whether there exist any ground for the above mentioned accusation. It seems to us that the people from SNPJ lost all sense of right judgment.

SLOVENIAN

Proletarec, Vol. 7, No. 536, Dec. 18, 1917.

CONFERENCE OF SLOVENIAN BENEVOLENT SOCIETIES
IN CHICAGO.

All Slovenian Benefit Societies located in Chicago and vicinity were invited to send their authorized representatives to a conference to be held on December 13.

The following societies answered this request:

"Narodni Vitezi" No.39
"Slavia" No. 1
"Slovenski Dom" No. 86
"Nada" No. 102
"Francisco Ferrer" No. 131
"Modern Woodmen"
"Slovenski Delavski Sokol"
"Slovenia" (Bohemian)
"Society No. 47"
"Society No. 1"
"Socialist Club No. 1"
"Singing Society--Zora"

"Jugosloven No. 104"
"Slovenian Youth Society--Danica--No. 70"

RADNICKA STRAZA, Vol. V. No. 42, October 3rd, 1912

A SOCIALIST CONVENTION

The SLOVENSKA NARODNA PODPORNA JEDNOTA (Slovenian National Benefit Union) decided at its fifth Convention, which was held in Milwaukee, Wisconsin to work for socialistic principles. Delegates of 10,600 members, who are scattered all over the United States will try to influence these members to work for the Socialist party and to join it or the Jugoslav Socialist branches or where such do not exist to organize them.

At the convention there were 120 delegates present, among them two from Mexico. Out of them 80 were members of some Socialist organization, while the rest of them side with socialism.

At the convention as the main speaker was Comrad EPPIGHIST.... His speech was well as of other Socialist speakers was received with great enthusiasm.

Proletareo, Vol. 3, No. 29, March 31, 1908.

SLOVENIAN BENEVOLENT SOCIETY "NADA"

The Slovenian women in Chicago have organized a new benevolent society called "Nada" (hope). Last Sunday, March 15th, twenty women signed applications for membership to this newly organized society.

A membership card costs $1.00. Monthly dues are $.50. The society will pay $3 a week for sick benefit, and $50 in case of death.

The Executive Board consists of:- Mary Jelich, President; Mary Grileo, Vice-President; Angela Norvat, Treasurer.

Controling Committee:- Ursula Koshnik, Mary Sottar, Anna Krizanich.

The Committee for the sick includes Mrs. Zavitnik and Mrs. Neden.

II. CONTRIBUTIONS
   AND ACTIVITIES
   D. Benevolent and Protective
      Institutions
      6. Settlement Houses and
         Community Centers

Majskiglas, (The May Herald), Vol. XVII, May 1937.

OUR INSTITUTIONS AND THEIR FUTURE

The Jugoslav Socialist Federation and its official publication, Pro-
letarec, the Educational Bureau of the Federation, the American Family
Almanac (Druzinski Koledar), the May Herald and the Home of the
Federation, the Slovene Labor Center.

We cannot escape the fact that the old generation of Slovenes will not
be with us forever, but their work, the institutions they built, are
with us to stay and are today facing a brighter future than ever.

The new generation of American-born Slovenes is gradually stepping
into the work which has up to the present time been carried on by
the old pioneers in the Socialist movement. This change, because of its
very nature, is bound to be slow at first, but as the young comrades
are gradually drawn into the movement and begin to take up the work

Majskiglas, Vol. XVII, May 1937.

and responsibility connected with it, interest will develop at a faster tempo than it has up to the present time.

The record back of the Jugoslav Socialist Federation is one of which we can feel justly proud. The official organ of the Federation, Proletarec, has survived all the storms of the last thirty-three years, many of which were terrific ones, and is today carrying on nobly. The English section of Proletarec is open to our youth and is gradually becoming more and more interesting as new contributors are being added to the list. The rapid tempo with which changes are taking place today among the working masses gives us hundreds of new topics to discuss and we should do so through our publication and in that way make it interesting enough to be able to attract new subscribers from the ranks of the youth.

Majskiglas, Vol. XVII, May 1937.

The Educational Bureau of the Jugoslav Socialist Federation has, accord-
ing to its secretary's report for the last year, more units affiliated
with it than ever before in the history of the Bureau.

New material is being constantly added to the bureau's files, more and
more calls for plays, declamations, etc. are being efficiently and
satisfactorily handled from month to month, and the future for the
Educational Bureau looks bright and prosperous. The Bureau, with its
fine and large collection of material, is today in a position whereby
it is able to be of great service to its affiliated units. Fraternal
and cultural organizations throughout the country are beginning to
realize this and new organizations are being added to the membership
list right along. English speaking units affiliated with the Bureau
will soon be furnished with a complete new list, which is now being

Majskiglas, Vol. XVII, May 1937.

compiled of all the English material in the files of the Bureau.

Our annual publication, the May Herald, dedicated to labor's international holiday, May Day, is being improved and enlarged from year to
year, this issue being one of which we are all proud and one which should
enjoy a large circulation.

The American Family Almanac, (Druzinski Koledar), is in its twenty-third
year with the 1937 issue. The contents and general make-up of the
Almanac have been improved with each issue and the circulation records
show that its list of readers is growing constantly. The research work
and gathering and publishing of statistics by its editor, dealing with
Slovenes and their activities in America, have made the Almanac a
valuable reference book much in demand by libraries and people doing
research work throughout the country.

The most recent and probably the best accomplishment of our Federation

Majskiglas, Vol. XVII, May 1937.

was the purchase, a few years ago, of the building which is now known
as the Sloveno Labor Center, or the Center, as it is known among the
Chicago Slovenes. The business office of Proletarec is located in
the building, as is the Proletarec Library and book shop. The Slovene
social Center Club, which has about three hundred members, is also
located at the Center. The building is located in a residential section,
away from the hustle and bustle of the city's traffic and industry, and
is the meeting place of all Jugoslav Socialist Federation members in
Chicago and of the out-of-town visitors. It is the Slovene Labor
Center in the full sense of the word.

Our movement has a home which can be called its own and of which we
can all feel justly proud.

The biggest and most important problems before the Federation today

Majskiglas, Vol. XVII, May 1937.

are: First, to increase our membership; this increase will have to come
from the ranks of youth; and second, to build up the circulation of our
official organ, Proletarec. The field in which we will have to do most
of our work is in and among the labor unions.

The most **vital** movement on the American scene today is the giant stir-
ring of the workers in the b sic industries. To guide this gigantic
force into really pro ressive channels among our people is the most
immediate task before the members of our Federation and its sympathizers.

Amerikanski Slovenec, Vol. XXXVII, No. 236, Dec. 11, 1928.

SLOVENSKI DOM

The management of our highly praised national institution Slovenski Dom
informs all organizations in Chicago that on account of low financial
conditions of this institution, it will be advisable to use its premises
for all kinds of celebrations, bazaars, theatrical performances, etc.,
which societies and lodges are planning to do.

With rent paid anywhere, we are lowering our support to this such helpful
important and altruistic institution, of which we have all be proud.

Amerikanski Slovenec, Vol. XXXV, No. 77, April 21, 1926

NEW SLOVENIAN HALL IN CHICAGO

Life of our colony in Chicago is getting into a new tempo. The cause of
this is that our new Slovenian Hall has been opened. Very soon this hall
will become a real center of our colony, where friends and relatives
will meet. This hall is located on the second floor of our St. Stephano's
church building. Its modern premises offer excellent surroundings for
social meetings. The hall is big enough to accommodate nearly 1,500 persons
and is always filled to the limit whenever some colonial gathering occurs.
In the basement of this building we can find two bowling alleys, where
hundreds of young and old people find enjoyment every evening, but especially on Sundays. All seats are occupied by the spectators. The church
treasury found an excellent source of steady income from this enterprise.
Next to the bowling room there is a pool room with a few brand new pool
tables. Our young people find there a good place to amuse themselves,
under the guidance of clergymen. The parents do not have to worry about
their children's conduct as long as they are closely watched by our
priests.

Amerikanski Slovenec, Vol. XXXV, No. 77, April 21, 1926.

Children must have amusement and if they do not have it at home, they
will soon be looking for it in some other places, where we never know
what may happen to them. This very important problem in the way of
protecting our children's morals is solved entirely by the opening of
our hall, which provides wholesome entertainments under the watchful
eyes of the priest and his assistants. We can say that St. Stephan's
Hall is really a blessing for the old and young in our colony.

Amerikanski Slovenec, Vol. XXXIV, No. 20, Feb. 5, 1925.

SLOVENE COMMUNITY HOUSE

At last we got good news that our hope came true, our Community House is almost ready to be open. We all know the great importance of having such a house. Our children will have airy rooms to play in; we will enjoy meetings with our friends; and at this house we will attend performances of our musical, singing and dramatic societies.

It is really a surprising fact that so many of our people cannot realize the priceless value of such enterprise and are refusing to subscribe to the Building Fund. We cannot improve our life unless we will readily donate for the educational organizations.

III. ASSIMILATION
    A. Segregation

SLOVENIAN

Proletarec, Vol. XXIV, No. 1128, April 25, 1929.

HERE AND THERE AMONG US IN CHICAGO

Often we glance back into the early days of childhood, dreaming of
how we used to run about as free as the air. Comparing those never-
to-be-forgotten days with the present, we say to ourselves, What
a change! For well do we remember the old Slovene settlement at
Twenty-second and Wood streets, when that settlement was in its prime,
when the industries were flourishing in the car shops, the lumber
yards, etc. The noon factory whistles would blow and a mass of
humanity would dash across Blue Island avenue into their favored
places with a pail called 'pint.' Today the noon whistles still
blow, but not nearly as many humans scamper across the street; the
stores of the avenue look deserted.

What a change in so short a time! Of course, the war came and out
of the war many hardships. Many disabled boys, many new millionaires
and a period of depression. That hit our people hard, no doubt.

Proletarec, Vol. XXIV, No. 1128, April 25, 1929.

Yes, new machinery, too, has been invented displacing men. Many
have moved to the west of the city; some to the north, others to
the south. Yet, the flow of Slovenes from other cities and places
in the most part from the mining districts, has refilled the
territory. As one leaves another comes.

Fifteen to twenty years is a long period of time, too. Within such
a period much can be accomplished. But it is regrettable that the
Slovenes in this vast metropolis have nothing outstanding to which
one might point with pride. They have fostered fraternal societies, ·
a church and church hall. Outside of a few small business under-
takings, we have little to show.

Our people have not been interested in politics, although they are
becoming more conscious politically each year. Those that did participate in politics, for the most part always favored the Democratic
and Republican administrations. Each year taxes would rise, jobs

SLOVENIAN

Proletarec, Vol. XXIV, No. 1128, April 25, 1929.

would be fewer and harder to secure. Living necessities do not balance
with the meager pay envelopes. So we struggle along just barely
making both ends meet. Yet, our Slovene race as a whole is a progressive race. However, when you   scrutinize their achievements, we
are outspoken. We have no big DOM to which we might point with
pride; no large business establishments; no cooperatives. Perhaps
we did not need them as bad as other large Slovene settlements.
It is because we have too many factions and let jealousy control
our progress. Or is it because we always leave it to the other
fellow to do the work? Whatever it may be, the fact remains that
much more could be accomplished if the slogan of cooperation was
inbedded in the mind and heart of our people.
Isn't it a fact that jealousy has been responsible for so small
a degree of success? Time and again folks would tell us about our
fraternal life; about the friction caused by mere jealousy - and
the organization of a new order wherein the years following. They
had witnessed the same jealousy segregate subordinate groups. The

Proletarec, Vol. XXIV, No. 1128, April 25, 1929.

same jealousy retards the growth of any group and ours is no exception.

Chicago has had a Slovene Socialist Club for a long time. During all these years and especially in the past fifteen years cultural work has been progressing at very slow rate. But a large percentage of what has been done in this field can be attributed to the efforts of the Socialist club. The club just naturally tackled the work and knowing the responsibility of such action, it marched along as best it could under our conditions. Plays of all descriptions have been produced, lectures on vital questions are held at frequent intervals, literature of all kinds is distributed, devotees of music and song display their wares with the club's choir.

Young friends, if you are at all active, or wish to become so, there is no better time than now to join the ranks of active Socialist workers. There is no need for you to remain outside of our ranks any longer and pass away the fleeting years in the mere satisfaction

Proletarec, Vol. XXIV, No. 1128, April 25, 1929.

of doing only what you must. Think of being able to help others.
You will find more satisfaction in that. Your ability and your
earnestness is wasted unless you give the world the best you
possess. We would like to see you learn more about the economical
conditions which have so much bearing on your environment.

It is possible to do more in the next fifteen years than in the
last fifteen. We believe so. We believe there are at least three
hundred Slovenes in Chicago who should rightfully be attached to
the Socialist club. It is possible with proper judgment and unity
to do something to which you can point with pride and satisfaction
in years to come.

Donald J. Lotrich.

III A
II B 2 f
I A 3

SLOVENIAN

Amerikanski Slovenec, Vol. XXXVII, No. 201, Oct. 18, 1928.

CITIZENSHIP SCHOOL IN SOUTH CHICAGO

In last week's issue, readers of _Amerikanski Slovenec_ can notice a very important announcement regarding a new citizenship school to be opened very soon in South Chicago. The organizing committee invites all Slovenian women and men in our colony to be present at the meeting, October 18, where plans for opening this school will be discussed. The main object of this long needed school is to educate people in ways and means of, becoming citizens of this country.

A great number of articles have been printed dealing with the important question of becoming citizens. Sincere and sensible advice has been passed on how to take part in political life in this country, but still the fact remains that our people are the most ignorant people of this country so far as politics are concerned. They accept bills, taxes, assessments, etc., without questioning their rightfulness or the size of their bills. They will be more careful if they had their citizenship and political education.

Amerikanski Slovenec, Vol. XXXVII, No. 173, Sept. 8, 1928.

FIRST DUTY OF CITIZEN

The greatest right of every citizen of this democratic country is the
vote. We are sorry to state that the majority of our people do not recognize the value of this right and fail to exercise this most important
duty. The result of this failure is political mischief. The public pays
a heavy penalty having the wrong kind of politicians and by lack of
understanding how important it is to vote. A great number of our Slovenians used to say, "I do not care for politics." This attitude is entirely
wrong and should be changed by political education.

People cannot have the right kind of government and cannot govern themselves
unless they take part in electing their political leaders, which in this
country can be accomplished only by a majority vote. Political influence
is so important in the life of every citizen that it is a crime to neglect
the duty of controling this widespread influence. We strongly advice our
people to get away from political lethargy and fully exercise their first
and chief duty as American citizens, by voting.

Amerikanski Slovenec, Vol. XXXV, No. 77, April 21, 1926.

SLOVENIAN SETTLEMENT LIFE

Our colony in Chicago is growing very fast. Reason for this is increasing
industrial activity. Daily we see some new faces.

Since we built a new church hall, every week some new entertainment is
offered to people of our colony. Singing societies, dramatic clubs, etc.,
are giving weekly performances with choices of programs. This hall
proved to be the best place to meet friends and relatives. It can
easily accommodate over 1,500 persons.

The opening of this modern hall is really a convincing fact of how
badly we needed such premises. In the basement of the hall we have
two bowling alleys and every evening you can find hundreds of people
watching the play. The church has a pretty good income from this
enterprise. In the room close to the bowling alleys we find a pool
table, which also serves as a means for additional income to the
church.

Amerikanski Slovenec, Vol. XXXV, No. 77, April 21, 1926.

Due to the improvement in working conditions we notice great building
and remodeling activities; new beautiful homes built by our people;
old ones are remodeled to such an extent that you hardly can recognize
them; new furniture is bought, and we see that our people are getting
the best from civilized life; to which they hardly have been accustomed
before their arrival in this country.

SLOVENIAN

Amerikanski Slovenec, Vol. XXXV, No. 5, Jan. 8, 1926.

CHICAGO COLONY IS GROWING FAST

The Slovenian colony in Chicago is growing surprisingly fast. For the last
few months more than 100 new families have settled. The reason is the
lack of opportunity for new and young generations in small towns. Chicago,
with its vast industries, offers an excellent chance for ambitious young
persons. Old Slovenian people, of course, feel badly in new surroundings
and find it very hard to adjust themselves, being mine workers practically
all their life.

The Slovenian colony has good schools, recreation halls, etc. All this
provides for good life.

III. ASSIMILATION
    B. Nationalistic
       Societies and influences
       2. Activities of Nationalistic
         Societies

Amerikanski Slovenec, Vol. XXXVII, No. 100, May 24, 1928. APA (IL) PROJ 30275

35TH ANNIVERSARY OF THE SOCIETY "KNIGHTS OF ST. FLORIAN"

May the 6th was a memorable day for members of the society "Knights of
St. Florian." On this day this oldest society in America celebrated its
35th anniversary.

Due to the wide influence of this society, the celebration turned to be
a mass meeting of thousands of members, sympathizers and other Slovenians
from Chicago and vicinity. We must admit that the celebration was a brilliant affair in our colony.

The banquet, with a selected menu, was beyond our expectation; the artistic
program of the singing society "Sarja"; recital, given by the young members
of this society and interesting speeches dealing with the colorful history
of this society. We are not writing history and therefore, in this article
we will omit details of the Society's activities during the period of 35
years; even if we felt that it would be of great benefit to our new generation to learn how to work and create glory for our nationality.

Amerikanski Slovenec, Vol. XXXV, No. 335, Dec. 4, 1926.

BRANCH OF THE SLOVENIAN WOMEN'S SOCIETY

December 1, 1926, will be memorable day in the life of our Slovenian
women. On that date the Slovenian Women's Society opens its branch in
Chicago. Not long ago our people just laughed at the idea of their
women being organized and show men's activity. It seems to be a very
hard job for our men to imagine their wives taking part in social and
cultural life, of our people. So, our women got out from their kitchens
and are now active in the colony's affairs.

On that day at 8 P. M. the first meeting was held in the premises of our
school. On this occasion over 35 members signed applications.

You should see the joy on their faces. The board of directors has been
elected and will consist of: President, Mrs. Fannie Jazbec; Secretary,
Mrs. Majda Brishar; Treasurer, Mrs. Jennie Stayer.

Decision has been passed that on day of December 19, they will call mass
meeting on which should be invited all women from our colony in Chicago
and vicinity. Rules and regulations of this society as well as plans for
future work will be worked out at the next meeting.

III. ASSIMILATION
    C. National
        Churches and Sects

Amerikanski Slovenec, Vol. XXXV, No. 136, July 16, 1926.

SLOVENIAN SECTION 28TH INTERNATIONAL EUCHARISTIC CONGRESS IN CHICAGO

The Slovenian Section 28th International Eucharistic Congress in Chicago
held a meeting on July 22nd in the School Hall of St. Stjefan. More than
300 representatives from numberless Slovenian colonies in America were
present.

The chairman of this Section, Rev. K. Zakrajshek, opened the meeting
with a selected speech, in which he openly accused our Slovenian
clergy of being selfish and of exploiting the church for their own
purposes."These priests' attitude," he said, "will rain good relationship and respect toward church leaders and cease religious feelings
in their parishes."

He advises all clergymen to pay more attention to the economic life
of their church members; work on their welfare, education, etc., and
bear in mind that the members of the church are already overcharged
with assessments. The church must be a place for peace of mind, not
for political or financial activities.

Amerikanski Slovenec, Vol. XXXIV, No. 147, Sept. 18, 1925.

SLOVENE CATHOLIC CONFERENCE IN SOUTH CHICAGO

Last Sunday, the 20th of September, should live a long time in our memory.
In that day our South Chicago was the place where the Slovenes' Catholic
conference held its inauguration. Thousands of members and friends of our
Catholic organizations came here and brought other thousands of their
relatives with them to be present and witness this great celebration. Such
or similar occasions, when people of our race gather together, is of great
importance to our life in this country. Long time friends, missing for
years or living apart in different places of America, found great joy in
seeing each other. Valuable for their existence,informations concerning
working conditions, customs, etc., have been exchanged. New acquaintances
and friendships have been developed. This occasion manifests our strong
desire for unity and has been marked by colorful celebrations which will
be remembered for a long time.

Amerikanski Slovenec, Vol. XXXIV, No. 137, Sept. 1, 1925.

IS THAT WHAT YOU CALL HONESTY?

The other day Martin Zeleznikar, president of the Slovenian National Benefit Society, issued a certain statement which is not as correct as it should
be.

He plainly announced that their organization is the biggest of its kind
in this country. We are not interested in his opinion nor jealous of their
organization's business or growth, but what really interests us and brought
his statement to our attention is his accusation of our fanaticism, as well
as his advice not to believe in the Roman God. We are not against religious
tolerance because, living in this free country, we are used to that, but
a broadcast of this nature, coming from a person of the Catholic faith, is
really surprising. Furthermore, we believe in everybody's liberty to
believe or not to believe in certain doctrines, and cannot approve Mr.
Zeleznikar's unholy propaganda, just to reject religion or faith in God
as something worthless and unnecessary for the life of our Slovene people.

<u>Amerikanski Slovenec</u>, Vol. XXXIV, No. 137, Sept. 1, 1925.

Mr. Zeleznikar and his followers from the Slovenian National Benefit Society
may believe that their society is really as big as the whole world, but this
opinion does not give them right to muscle into other people's faith, nor
have they the authority to question the masses's belief in God. Being
members or even leaders of a big national organization does not make them
big enough to absorb or fully understand religious ideals and doctrines.

<u>Amerikanski Slovenec</u> and its followers will guard their unbroken faith
and will fight for their religious ideas to the last limit.

Proletarec, Dec. 11, 1918.

PIOUS CLERICALISM

Religious sentiment is not very deeply rooted in the human soul, but a certain class of people is trying its best to develop this feeling in order to exploit it. Often churches are built, religious customs invented, babies baptized, not to create by all this a religious and pious feeling, but in most cases to provide a fine living for priests, popes, clerics, rabbis, etc.

Clerics are using this pious sentiment as a means of gaining power over the people's souls as well as a means of dominating their pocketbooks. An unholy desire to live well, and a rebellion against progress is cleverly hidden under the robes of the church attendants, by banners, a church press, talks, ceremonies, observance of customs, etc.

Clerics do not even hesitate to use political power by organizing, or supporting, political organizations. To live well is the secret desire of clericalism, by

now a most powerful organization. Anyone who feels deep down in his heart
a cultural and moral sense of responsibility must resist this unholy power.

It is the fast growing and firm opinion of the thinking masses that clericalism
is nothing more than an open wound on the body of cultural and intellectual
life. This wound has become infected by now, and anybody serving the purpose
of clericalism is nothing but a parasite.

We find a number of reasons cited by the anti-clerical front in its fight on
clericalism. Some of these are false pretenses of being pious by the clerics,
a strong but masked desire to achieve power over the souls of the people, with
the purpose of collecting for a comfortable living.

On the other hand, we find the argument advanced that Rome, together with the
rest of clericalism, is the worst enemy of our people's church.

Finally, the worst misrepresentation of Christ's teachings is seen in the

Proletarec, Dec. 11, 1918.

clerical life, customs, ceremonies, etc.

There seems to be a strong fundamental truth in each one of these opinions.

Organizations

III E
II B 3
III B 2
I C

Amerikanski Slovenec, Vol. XXXII, No. 131, July 8, 1929.

GIRL EAGLES MEET

The Slovenian Eagles from our largest colony in America, Cleveland, Ohio, arrived here today under the leadership of their spiritual leader, Rev. Father M. Jager, assistant pastor in the Slovenian church there.

This evening in Czech-American Hall, 1440 W. 18th St., they will meet and exhibit their drills and other calisthenics, which will interest all. It is needless to say that we expect all Slovenes, young and old, to be present and our cordial invitation is extended.

An especially hearty welcome to our Cleveland visitors who are honoring us with their contribution.

The Slovenian Orel (Eagles) have had no better chance to show their accomplishments than they have today in Chicago, and tomorrow at the

- C

SLOVENIAN

Amerikanski Slovenec, Vol. XXXIII, No. 171, July C, 1926.

all-Slavic congress at Lemont, Ill. Never before had the American Slovenes an opportunity to witness such a glorious performance in their adopted country.

The Slovenian Orel is a purely Slovenian institution. The Orel organisation is a Slovenian national school out of which the people and church may get something mighty and of great significance.

We need a pure, single character here as well as in the old country. The old country needs it to suppress a continuous wall of foreign propaganda which is denationalizing and irreligious, and which aims to swallow us when we are nationally and politically weak.

More than ever, here in America, we need a national Catholic Slovenian character. Anybody that wants to, can see how anti-Slovenian evangelists are misleading (us). Here is where we need a revival of our characteristics! How?

- 3 -

Amerikanski Slovenec, Vol. XXXII, No. 131, July 8, 1929.

The American-Slovenian generation, born and raised in America, is getting more numerous from year to year. This young generation is here and ready to take over our organizations, lodges, clubs, parishes, in fact all that is ours. In ten years this new generation will reach maturity and our American-Slovenian institutions will naturally fall on their shoulders.

Now the question is How much is this young generation Slovenian in national and religious spirit? How are the families and individuals? Responsibility lies with leadership.

Against americanization there is no remedy; that we are in the melting pot there is no question, but there is no sufficient reason why we go so fast.

A great help to preserve our national and religious spirit is derived from Slovenian organizations. Among the first ones is the Orel (Eagles)

- 4 -

Ameriknski Slovenec, Vol. XXXIII, No. 131, July 6, 1920.

organization. The purpose of the organization is obvious. It wants to
raise strong national and religious characters. With athletics and physical education, Catholic in spirit, raising them in a Christian faith,
leading them regularly to receive sacraments, where Greis with faith
in God are prepared for the fullest life, and are the most competent for
leadership.

III. ASSIMILATION
    H. Relations
        with Homeland

Amerikanski Slovenec, Vol. XXXV, No. 15, Jan. 22, 1926.

PROTEST MEETING

Following an invitation from the president of K. S. K., Mr. Anton Grdina, thousands of our people in Chicago came to hear speakers on the 18th of January, 1926. The general purpose of this call was to send a protest against the injustice done in Jugoslavia to our people in Slovenia. A committee to collect means to help our people in the old country has been formed from distinguished members of this colony.

In this noble action our Slovenian women's organizations show great success, by organizing all kinds of entertainments and contributing large sums of money to support the above mentioned action. Last Sunday our Slovenian Women's Benefit Society held its annual carnival, which is already pronounced a great success from moral and material standpoints.

Such attitude toward problems of our needy people deserves high praise and encouragement. We people of Slovenian extraction, must help each other if we want to survive the hard times.

Proletarec, Vol. 14, No. 496, Feb. 12, 1919.

SLOVENIAN APPEALS.

The Central Committee of the Slovenian Republican Organization (Slovenian Republican Zveza) sent the following telegram to President Wilson:

> United States President, Woodrow Wilson
> Paris, France.

The Slovenian Republican Alliance, representing an overwhelming majority of Slovenes in America, who faithfully followed your standard and have with untold sacrifice supported your principles, appeal to you at the request of hundreds of Slovenian societies for protection of the Jugoslav rights at the peace conference.

To hand over visibly Slovene and Croatian regions to a foreign rule would mean a painful injustice and great danger for the future. Jugoslavs, who admire your democratic consistency, believe in you and appeal in this critical hour for justice. Exceedingly grateful to you for everything you have done for the rights of nations, and with the fact in mind that million of eyes are cast upon you, we, the Jugoslavs

Proletarec, Vol. 14, No. 496, Feb. 12, 1919.

beg you not to forget them in this hour of determination.

Etain Kristan, Chairman
A. J. Terbovec, Secretary

Monsieur Clemenceau
President de la Conference
Du Paix,
Paris, France.

The Slovenian Republican Alliance, representing an overwhelming majority of Slovenes living in America, who have at all times truly and with great sacrifices supported the cause of democracy, appeal at the request of hundreds of organizations to the peace conference for the consideration of the Jugoslav rights with justice.

To yield regions inhabited by a visible Jugoslav population to a foreign government would hew into the Jugoslavs a burning wound and establish great danger for the future. In the name of democracy, in the name of peace, and in the name of liberty, brotherhood, and equality, we beg of you, justice.

Etain Kristan, Chairman   A. J. Terbovec, Secretary

Proleturec, Vol. 14, No. 590, Jan. 1, 1919.

MILLION DOLLAR FUND FOR SLAVIC LIBERTY.

At the regular meeting of the Central Committee of the Slovenian Republican Organization it has been decided to organize a subscription and collect donations for a Million Dollar Fund, with which our people can be freed from the Italian annexation. The figure of a million dollars may sound enormous and alarming, but after all, it is worth the cause we are fighting for; and if we can judge from the number of sympathizers, we believe the figure will be easily attained.

The following emblems will be distributed among subscribers:
Five dollars will have an emblem bearing the initials S. R. O.
From five dollars to ten dollars, a similar emblem with one star.
From ten to twenty-five dollars, an emblem with two stars.
From twenty-five to fifty dollars, an emblem with three stars.

Artistic Diplomas will also be awarded to those who will subscribe from twenty-five to fifty dollars.

Proletarec, Vol. 13, No. 586, Dec. 4, 1918.

MANIFEST MEETING OF CHICAGO SLOVENES.

On November 28, 1918 several of the Slovenian organizations, such as the Slovenes Republican Organization and branches of Slovenian women organizations, called a mass meeting at Pilsen Auditorium.

The main purpose of this meeting was to protest against the Italian aspiration to annex Jugoslavian sea-borders.

The meeting was called to order by Frank Zaitz, who explained the purpose of the meeting and read the resolution, which was signed by thirty thousand Slovenians and will be transmitted to President Wilson.

A few excellent speakers offered lectures on the question of Slovenian and Jugo-slavian integrity and their right to decide the future of their people, living on the Jugoslavian border, which the present Italian government is trying to occupy. All speakers pointed out the strong wish of the Slovenian people abroad to keep their independence. They expressed their hope that America, in accordance with the

Proletarec, Vol. 13, No. 536, Dec. 4, 1918.

Peace Conference Policy, will protect the minority.

F. Zaitz also read an appeal, which has been transmitted to a number of administrative and political bodies, asking support in the Slovenian resistance to annexation. The Slovenes from all political factions agreed to work shoulder to shoulder on this important question of Slovene liberty.

The Slovenes, who attended this meeting expressed their strong protest against the London Pact, which permitted the Italians to occupy the Jugoslavian border.

In order to cover expenses to transmit the appeals and pay rent for the hall, the people collected the sum of $63.30.

Great hope for President Wilson's intervention in this grave situation prevailed.

INDIVIDUALS

<u>Proletarec</u>, Apr. 28, 1932.

DR. OTIS M. WALTER

Dr. Otis M. Walter, one of the most prominent Slovenian physicians and surgeons on the West Side of Chicago, will celebrate a rare accomplishment. It was exactly twenty years ago May 1, that the doctor established his office on Twenty-sixth Street and Crawford Avenue.

At that time, the vicinity was not developed to the extent that it is today. One little room comprised his whole office. As the years rolled on, the doctor annexed larger quarters and installed modern medical equipment. All types and nationalities of people trekked to him, and his fame as a surgeon spread rapidly, as one after another of the many patients successfully overcame the most serious complications and illnesses, and his ability as a surgeon became known.

From that same location, the doctor has been serving the people of this
community continuously during these twenty years. No worker, unable
to pay for treatment or surgery work, has ever been turned away.

The doctor has been an instructor in schools and colleges prior to the
beginning of his present professional career, and even after entry
into private business, he has been experimenting and developing new
and modern methods of surgical and medical procedures. For the past
thirteen years he has been a member of the surgical staff of the Francis
Willard Hospital, and for the past ten years a member of the surgical
staff of the North Chicago Hospital. Dr. O. M. Walter is well-known
among the Jugo-Slavs of this city. When asked to what he attributes
his success, he is firm in saying "to the Slavic people."

It is indeed a coincidence that the doctor should have reason, to celebrate on the day of all days, May 1, and it is our hope that he may live
many more years, and assist the workers as he has heretofore.